The Small Business Owner's Handbook to

SEARCH ENGINE OPTIMIZATION

Increase Your Google Rankings, Double Your Site Traffic...

In Just 15 Steps - Guaranteed

Stephen Woessner

Search Engine

uble Your Site

Traffic...In Just

Copyright © 2009 Stephen Woessner

Published by Atlantic Publishing Group, Inc.

1405 SW 6th Ave. • Ocala, FL 34471-0640 • PH 800-814-1132 • FAX 352-622-1875

Web site: www.atlantic-pub.com • E-mail sales@atlantic-pub.com

SAN Number: 268-1250

ISBN-13: 978-1-60138-443-0

Library of Congress Cataloging-in-Publication Data

Woessner, Stephen, 1972-
The small business owner's handbook to search engine optimization : increase your Google rankings, double your site traffic-- in just 15 steps--guaranteed / by Stephen Woessner.
      p. cm.
Includes bibliographical references and index.
ISBN-13: 978-1-60138-443-0 (alk. paper)
ISBN-10: 1-60138-443-2 (alk. paper)
1. Small business--Computer network resources. 2. Search engines. 3. Google (Firm) I. Title.
HD2341.W56 2009
658.8'72--dc22

                              2009027946

COVER & INTERIOR DESIGN: Meg Buchner • megadesn@mchsi.com

Printed in the United States

CONTENTS

Chapter 3
Become Google-Friendly   **65**

Chapter 4
Strategic and Tactical Keyword Selection   **81**

Chapter 5
Optimize Your Site's Code 109

Chapter 6
Optimize Your Site's Page Content 141

Chapter 7
Accelerate Rankings with Link Building 171

DEDICATION

My very first thank you and words of appreciation have to go to my wife, Christine, and our 2-year-old daughter, Caitlyn. This project was incredibly difficult and time-consuming because it was my first book. I have written many papers and research studies, but never something of this magnitude. Consequently, I spent many weekends and evenings tucked away in our home office writing this book instead of playing with Caitlyn or spending quality time with family and friends. There are trade-offs to everything in life; however, the amount of time I invested toward this book was much more than I ever imagined at the onset. The understanding I received from Christine and Caitlyn made the long hours bearable. I am blessed to have special people in my life who have always loved me. Thank you, my love.

Another special thank you goes to my mother, Evie Riegler. She has always wanted the best for me and encouraged me to think and dream big. She has been proud of me during my times of triumph and assured me that things would be okay during my times of failure. My mother has also been my coach and mentor. I still remember the seemingly endless rehearsals we would do before the annual speech and poetry competition at my elementary school (Heritage Christian School in Canton, Ohio). She never demanded that I be the best; however, she coached me to practice so I could apply all of my talents. Those invaluable rehearsal sessions gave me the skills I needed to become comfortable working in front of, and with, large groups of people. I still rely on those skills today at the university. My mother, as well as my entire family, always embraced the concept of hard work, dedication, commitment to one another, and an intense entrepreneurial spirit. These values shaped who I have become today.

I would also like to thank several of my best friends for their ongoing support and motivation when I didn't think I would actually get this project completed on time. The advice I received from Greg Filbeck, Ted Stein, and Mitch Moths was invaluable. Their unbiased reviews of my writing and honest critiques of my business strategies were critically important. They continue to keep me grounded and focused on the goals ahead. Thanks guys.

I also need to thank my good friend and mentor, Tony Parinello. Tony is the *Wall Street Journal* best-selling author of *Selling to VITO* and has sold over one million books throughout his impressive career. Tony mentored me through the adventure of writing and promoting this book. Thank you, Tony, for your advice and expertise along this journey I decided to travel. I will never forget your generosity. I sincerely appreciate your help and encouragement.

I would also like to thank Douglas Brown and his team at Atlantic Publishing for taking a chance on me. They took a risk on an unproven and first-time author. I hope I don't let you down! And a special thank you to Meg Buchner at Atlantic. Meg is a former business partner of mine and the person who first introduced me to Douglas. She is also the outstanding graphic designer who designed my book cover. Thank you, Meg, for doing an amazing job. You're awesome!

Author Stephen Woessner

I have an intimate understanding of the challenges and obstacles faced by small business owners because I come from a family of hard-working entrepreneurs. My grandfather (Pop) immigrated to the United States from Greece in the early 1920s. He worked as a dishwasher in a small Canton, Ohio restaurant until he had saved enough money to open his own place. He named his first restaurant "The Ideal." Pop's business savvy and discipline would make any corporate executive envious. He managed to keep his restaurant afloat through the Great Depression by selling soup-and-sandwich combos for a nickel. How's that for a value menu? Pop's business plan was simple, "No matter how bad the economy gets…just remember… everyone's got to eat."

And he was right. Pop went on to open a larger restaurant called "The Colonial," which is still fondly remembered in Canton to this day. He passed down his unwavering work ethic to his son and three daughters, and then later, to his ten grandchildren.

My mother, one of Pop's daughters, owned a successful bakery and catering business for 14 years in North Canton until her health deteriorated and she was forced to close it. Former customers still rave about her elegant wedding cakes, pies, and decadent desserts. Her designs were unlike anything ever seen before, or since.

Three of my uncles owned amazingly popular restaurants, and two of my cousins currently own a gourmet chocolate company that consistently sells out its inventory on Home Shopping Network (HSN).

I too have owned several businesses — four to be exact. One of which made me a multi-millionaire by the time I was 28 years old. It was a dot-com named Fortified Nutrition. Fortified was a great idea, but was on a collision course with terrible timing. My management team and I quickly built the company up to a valuation of $10 million. Fortified enjoyed significant success as a result of its search engine optimization, viral marketing, online partnerships, affiliate marketing, and e-mail marketing strategies. We raised venture capital and obtained commercial financing from Wells Fargo.

Fortified planned to execute an initial public offering (IPO) in late 2001. However, our plans changed drastically when the dot-com bubble burst. I was in San Francisco negotiating with investors when the NASDAQ began its collapse. The multi-million-dollar value of my Fortified stock evaporated in what seemed an instant, and I lost over $100,000 of my own cash. My wife and I nearly lost everything.

Thankfully, the other three businesses provided decent returns. In 2006, I left the private sector and accepted a position at the University of Wisconsin's La Crosse Small Business Development Center (SBDC). Our SBDC is one of nearly 1,000 centers across the United States and its territories. Our sole purpose is to help small business owners like you start up, expand, and grow their companies through free business advising services and non-credit business education programs.

I oversee all non-credit business education programs on the University of Wisconsin-La Crosse campus. I also teach classes on search engine optimization, increasing online conversion rates, and sales strategies. In addition, I focus a portion of my time toward scholarly research in e-commerce, strategic marketing, and finance.

So how am I qualified to write this book? Here are some highlights:

- Built a successful search engine optimization model based on hundreds of research hours in both private-sector and academic settings

- Have more than 13 years of private-sector Web strategy and site development experience

- Have consulted with hundreds of clients on Web strategy and site development

- Built Fortified Nutrition to a valuation of $10 million and planned an IPO

- Teach wildly popular search engine optimization, online conversion rate, and sales training classes at the University of Wisconsin-La Crosse

- Have a successful track record of scholarly research and academic journal publication — most recent paper analyzed entrepreneurship within Second Life, a popular virtual world. The paper was published in the Journal of E-business.

In addition, I have a proven track record for successfully developing strategic and tactical solutions to problems in as little time as possible. My mantra in life is to work smarter, not harder. Consequently, my goal is to always maximize efficiency and effectiveness. I learned early on in my career that I had a gift for rapidly dissecting how a system worked, and once I understood the operation, I could quickly troubleshoot the relevant decision-making data to create a problem-solving solution — and typically in less time than my peers. I first recognized this gift while serving in the Air Force following my high-school graduation.

I like to tell stories, so I will illustrate my life-long pursuit of efficiency and effectiveness with the first of several stories that I share inside this book. I decided to share this story because I placed efficiency and effectiveness at the core of my SEO process.

I was a highly trained missile facilities technician for the Minuteman II Intercontinental Ballistic Missile System (long-range nuclear missiles, for short). My assigned team chief and I were responsible for the power and environmental systems for 150 nuclear missile silos located deep in the prairies of western South Dakota. A typical day at the "office" for me involved working 14 to 17 hours at a depth of 40 to 100 feet below ground level within extreme proximity to a huge nuclear warhead.

Most of our work was performed within what is called a "no-lone zone." Meaning we always had to be within eye-sight of our own team members to ensure security protocols. Everyone working in the missile field possessed a secret clearance or higher. Every day was literally a troubleshooting adventure, and none were the same as the last. It was an awesome experience, and it served as the ideal laboratory for me to first identify, and later perfect, my gift for increasing efficiency and effectiveness.

After about six months of "running the field," I earned my master-level technician status. I prided myself on my technical competency and would frequently challenge, and often win, debates with 15- to 20-year veterans on complicated system problems experienced within our various missile silos. I was continually on the outlook for the next big challenge that would truly test me. And then I got the call to take my ultimate test one summer weekend in 1992.

I was relaxing with my girlfriend — now my wife — and her family at their house in Rapid City, South Dakota. My emergency beeper went off and jolted me back to reality. I immediately called our Job Control Center at Ellsworth Air Force Base and was stunned at the reason for being summoned by the beeper. Job Control had received some startling news. "Airman Woessner, we have an alarm indicating there is a fire inside one of our silos, and we need you and Sergeant Andrews to dispatch immediately and take control of the situation." I was stunned. My initial thought was, "Why in the world are you calling me? I don't put out fires! I keep the silo running at full power and within the right temperature. Perhaps a different department could be of better service. Hey, thanks for beeping me, Job Control, but I have to get back to relaxing...click."

I of course did not say any of that, and when I snapped back to reality, I was told that the silo was running on emergency power, and because of that, the situation specifically fell within my area of expertise. Perfect.

I quickly kissed my girlfriend goodbye, ran out her front door, jumped into my black Nissan Pulsar SE NX (nice ride for a 20-year-old back in the day), and burned some Goodyear ST rubber back to the base. My mind was racing just about as fast as I was driving. I slid the Pulsar into our squadron's parking lot, hopped out, and sprinted inside our operations hangar to find my team chief and shop supervisor as quickly as possible.

My team chief — also named Steve — and I then packed and loaded our gear into our field truck, including air masks and oxygen tanks — which we typically did not carry. We were then carefully briefed by our supervisors regarding what we might encounter inside the silo. However, there were so many unknown conditions that it was difficult to devise a solid plan. We truly did not know what to expect, and I tend to dislike ambiguity. Our last order of business before departing base was to pick up our two-person armed escort, who would ride with us to the silo to ensure we arrived safely. They would also maintain a security perimeter above ground while we dealt with the situation inside the silo, below ground.

Let me take a second to paint the picture a bit more clearly. Our Minuteman II nuclear missile silos essentially consisted of two circular rooms located about 40 feet below ground level. Within the center of the two circular rooms sat a 100-foot-deep launch tube that was 12 feet in diameter. And in the center of the launch tube — yep, you guessed it — sat a mean, nasty nuclear warhead mounted on top of literally tons of solid rocket propellant. It can be an intimidating thing to see. Now, it does not take a rocket scientist or nuclear physicist to quickly calculate the danger in mixing fire with a nuclear warhead sitting on top of rocket propellant. This is not the recipe I had envisioned for a perfect summer weekend in South Dakota's Black Hills. I had been in tight situations inside several silos before, although never a legitimate life-and-death situation. This one was shaping up to be a much different, and more dangerous, challenge. I was going to get every ounce of the test I had been craving. As the reality of the situation sunk in, I started to get scared. And the excruciatingly long drive across the South Dakota prairie to the silo did not help.

In truth, I was having real difficulty focusing on the task at hand. A flood of emotions was crashing over me like a tidal wave. I knew Steve and I had to be fast. And we had to be accurate. We had to do our jobs without hesitation, because there was no time to waste. And there was definitely no margin for error. I knew this emergency was going to test my skill to work efficiently and effectively like nothing I had experienced before. It was the ideal opportunity to showcase what I had learned, and hopefully, I would not get blown up in the process. But did I have the courage to do this? Could I react and not hesitate? We were about to find out.

Again, we had only received generalities of what we might encounter once we entered the silo. The briefing details were general because the alarm being reported back to base was an all-or-nothing fire alarm. We had very limited decision-making data. Consequently, we did not have any confirmation of whether a fire was already raging inside the silo, which would significantly increase the probability of a serious situation occurring. Aside from the danger of the rocket fully igniting, the heat from the fire would also threaten the stability of the nuclear warhead itself. Our teams were typically responsible for keeping the missile silos cool and, specifically the warhead, within very strict tolerances of plus or minus a few degrees. The heat from a fire could lead to all sorts of serious problems. My head was beginning to spin with too many variables. On the other hand, maybe we would only encounter some minor smoke inside the silo and we could quickly neutralize the source.

To make matters worse, since the silo was underground, we would have to be directly on top of the silo before we could begin collecting data to help indicate what sort of situation we were up against. My heart was throbbing and my breathing was getting heavy. Were we about to become the next top story on 60 Minutes?

We finally arrived at the silo, and our armed escorts jumped out of the truck and did their jobs flawlessly. Steve and I executed our entrance protocols, authenticated our security codes with the assigned launch control center, and then assumed control and responsibility of the missile silo. Our next step was for us to stand at ground level directly above the missile for 30 minutes while the security door opened... slowly. The door timers are set to 30 minutes so that if hostiles were to take control of a missile silo, they too would have to wait 30 minutes for the door to open. In the meantime, additional security could be dispatched to regain control of the attacked silo. Theoretically, this is an excellent strategy to ensure silo security. However, I would have done just about anything for that door to have opened faster.

Steve and I had our equipment packs ready. We had strapped on our oxygen tanks and were now breathing through our air masks. As soon as the security door opened, we planned to climb down the 40-foot ladder, rush into the silo, and begin our troubleshooting process. As I stood there waiting, I had scenes from the movie Backdraft running through my head. I thought that, at any moment, I would hear air being sucked into the silo, igniting a stagnant fire, which would have been followed by a tremendously large, hideous explosion. That would have been lights out for us. Boom. I shook my head and laughed. My day was not improving as I had more time to think.

When the security door was finally open, I gave Steve a quick look for permission with my signature wry smile. He knew I was anxious, and he also knew that I desperately wanted to go into the silo first. He gave me the green light by giving me an energetic thumbs-up signal and yelling "Gooooooo!" Excellent...the action was finally on. I turned toward the silo's access shaft, my blood pressure spiked, and then I disappeared in an instant down into the silo. Did I actually use the ladder rungs, or did I just drop

40 feet? I honestly don't remember. I reached the first level of the silo in what seemed to be a millisecond. I stood, turned, and yelled "clear!" back up to Steve, who was waiting at ground level for my signal. He then moved down the ladder with the same efficiency I had demonstrated just seconds earlier. We both turned and rushed into the silo together. We immediately encountered the smoke. The silo was hazy, and it was challenging to see inside the first-level room.

This was not an encouraging scene. Was my heart pounding harder now? How was that even possible? Steve and I needed to find a solution fast! And now we were standing just six feet from a nuclear warhead, and all indications pointed to a fire somewhere in one of the silo's two rooms. But we had no idea where to look first, and we had limited visibility.

Then Steve and I remembered that during our pre-dispatch briefing, we had learned that the silo had switched over to emergency power temporarily for some unknown reason. This critically important clue intuitively led us to seek out the emergency generator on the second-level of the silo. It took what seemed forever to get there because we had to negotiate another ladder that we couldn't see very well. But we finally made it to the generator, and bingo! The motor inside the generator was beginning to burn and billowing out the smoke. The generator would soon be in flames unless we took immediate action. Steve and I quickly executed the silo shut-down procedures, which stabilized the situation and eliminated the danger.

Whoa. I put my hands on my hips and took several huge, labored breaths inside my mask. "Man, this job really rocks!!" I thought.

Total time troubleshooting in the silo was an impressive five minutes. How's that for maximizing efficiency and effectiveness?

Steve and I went back to ground level to decompress. Steve called in the details and results back to our Job Control Center on base. I took a walk to try and control my thoughts and stabilize my emotions. My veins were oozing with adrenaline. It was an incredible feeling. It would take me days to decompress from the high! I was only 20 years old and had just engineered a solution with Steve that mitigated a potential large-scale disaster. Now, that was exhilarating! The emergency at the silo had put my efficiency and effectiveness skills to the test during a real pressure cooker of a situation. There was absolutely no margin for error, and we passed with flying colors. My confidence, which I carried with me throughout the remainder of my enlistment, grew exponentially. Anything was possible now.

During my four years of military service, I successfully managed my Air Force responsibilities, carried a full-time course load as an undergraduate business student at Black Hills State University, held a part-time job off base to earn extra money, and still had time for a social life. I was honorably discharged in June 1994. My resume of accomplishments included two college degrees (Black Hills State University and The Community College of the Air Force); the National Service Defense Medal, Good Conduct Medal, and Outstanding Unit Award; and numerous certificates for technical competency, including my squadron's *Work Smarter – Not Harder* Award.

I believe receiving the *Work Smarter – Not Harder* Award validates my goal for maximizing efficiency and effectiveness in all of the projects I pursue. I accomplish this goal by following three simple guidelines that I have placed at the core of my SEO process: 1) develop a strategy, 2) develop a process, and then 3) execute flawlessly. These guidelines truly form the structure of the 15-step SEO process you are about to learn.

I also have a bachelor's of science in marketing from the University of Wisconsin-La Crosse and am finishing my master's in Business Administration (MBA) there as well. In addition to my work at the university, I serve on several non-profit boards, including Big Brothers Big Sisters of the 7 Rivers Region, the Onalaska Area Business Association, Workforce Development Board, and the Riverfront Inc. Foundation. You can find me on Facebook, LinkedIn, and Twitter.

I shared all this with you because I think it is important for you to know a little about me so you can be confident that I understand small business and the constraints you deal with every day, and that my experience can help you achieve efficiency and effectiveness. Rest assured, my SEO process will positively impact your bottom line. And if you are like most small business owners, cash and time constraints tend to be the most significant challenges you face most often. **Cash and time are two assets you can never have too much of — and my SEO process can give you more of both.**

My 15-step SEO process is effective at driving more traffic to a Web site and is simple and efficient to implement. And I back up your results with my 110 percent money back guarantee. You can read all about the guarantee in Chapter 2.

With that said, let us get started.

CHAPTER 1

The Small Business Owner SEO Briefing

Introduction and FAQs

I have consulted with many small business owners throughout my private-sector career and at the University of Wisconsin-La Crosse regarding a variety of Web-related topics, including search engine optimization (SEO). I can confidently say that the vast majority of the business owners I have worked with had the perception going into our meetings that SEO was inherently complicated and challenging from a technical perspective, and that it may be best if SEO were left to programmers.

I should probably confess I had a similar perception before I made the conscious decision to invest whatever time and effort it took to become an SEO expert. Before I began my SEO education, the thought of unlocking all of the coding mysteries and secret database tricks was intimidating. I envisioned the process would be like trying to solve the mysteries of the Dead Sea scrolls, or something just as tedious. And I had nearly ten years of Web-related experience at that point.

To make matters worse, I lacked a sense of confidence as I began to teach myself SEO, because my expertise is in the discipline of marketing. My private-sector experience, educational background, and current work at UW-La Crosse all point to marketing. My expertise is not in computer science or programming, despite having engineered the launch of FortifiedNutrition.com during the dot-com boom. I doubted that I had the requisite technical skills to master SEO, but I began what I feared to be an ill-fated journey nonetheless.

To my surprise, I discovered becoming skillful in SEO is more closely aligned to marketing than it is to computer science. In fact, SEO has little to do with programming or writing code. Instead of my 16 years of marketing experience holding me back, I found that it was going to give me a significant edge in SEO — much more so than any Web-related technical skills I had learned along the way — because over the course of my career, I had developed the ability to think like my customers, or, when I was a consultant, like my clients' customers. This is a critical skill when selecting awesome keywords because you need to get into the heads of your customers to identify the keywords that are used most frequently to find content like yours on the Internet. I will explain my entire keyword selection process in detail in Chapter 4. It is not as difficult as some SEO books and blogs would lead you to believe.

Now back to my SEO education process. I began by reading books, blogs, and Web sites. I suspect that most people do this same thing. I love to read, but I found this exercise to be tedious and time consuming because there is so much information devoted to SEO. I found myself spending hours wading through so much literature, and often, the sources contradicted themselves. The beginning of my SEO education was frustrating.

The core reason for my frustration at the early stages of this process was that I could not find any sources that did a good job of explaining the full process of optimizing a Web site in a step-by-step format. I found a relevant bit from one source and then another relevant bit from another source, but never one comprehensive source. Plus, none of the sources I found provided recommendations that could also maximize effectiveness and efficiency from the perspective of a small business owner — i.e., I did not want to devote my life to practicing SEO. I wanted to optimize a Web site and then move on with something else in life.

I also felt like the books I was studying were not written for me. It was as if the books had been written by programming professionals for other programmers. I also found the opposite extreme to be true occasionally, where the content was so elementary that it was not useful. The ultimate frustration was when I found what seemed to be a good recommendation, but then realized only about 50 percent of a process was being made available, with the remaining steps available for purchase on their Web site. And finally, I read some books where it seemed like their only purpose was promoting the author's SEO consulting business, as opposed to providing legitimate education for the reader.

I had gleaned as much as I could from the eclectic pile of references I had scoured. Then I ditched the printed material and opted instead for hands-on testing, because I love to experiment. It is one of my favorite ways to learn. So I developed some theories, collected some baseline data before beginning the tests, and launched some optimized Web site pages to see what would happen. To my surprise, the tactics I had applied in this initial round of tests seemed to work well. So I went back to the tactics, evolved them into a more formal process with a series of steps, made adjustments to the test pages, and re-launched, which lead to more success. The pages I had optimized actually doubled the number of monthly unique visitors who accessed the test site (monthly unique visitors is the only Web statistic that matters — more on that later) within just 30 days. I was ecstatic.

Although these initial results were encouraging, I had to temper my enthusiasm because much of the reading I had devoured warned me that Google had a reputation among SEO experts for changing their methods for indexing — or cataloging — content on the Internet. Essentially, "what worked today may be obsolete tomorrow" was the mantra. I had invested considerable time and energy up to this point developing an expertise in SEO that might become obsolete. I began to question whether the SEO process in my experiments would stand up over time, or would be rendered useless within a few months.

I can say confidently that the process has stood the test of time. The process is still intact and generating outstanding results. I recently finished optimizing a page on the UW-La Crosse Small Business Development Center Web site for our Certified Global Business Professional (CGBP) Series (**www.uwlax.edu/sbdc**), and the page scored three Top 10 rankings in Google, including a No. 8 ranking within 30 days. Plus, our CGBP page is competing against 60 million other pages in Google. Not bad for about one hour of work. I am going to teach you how to achieve the same or better results with your own Web site.

It is definitely true that Google changes their methods. However, as you will find out while studying this book, my 15-step process is based on high-quality techniques that benefit both Google and Web site visitors. I am going to teach you how to develop high-quality content pages — with no gimmicks or tricks — that your visitors will appreciate. When Google alters their methods, they are often working to eliminate what are called "Black Hat SEO tactics" and penalize the sites using the tactics. My SEO process does not include any Black Hat tactics. Instead, we will focus on developing high-quality well-optimized content, as well as building the popularity of your Web site. If you implement my 15-step process, you will safely increase your rankings, double your site traffic, and never have to fear being blacklisted and removed from Google's listings.

As I mentioned in my brief biography, I teach a wildly popular

SEO class at the UW-La Crosse titled Best Tactics for Online Marketing. The business owners who attend are surprised and relieved when I share the revelation that in order to be successful at SEO, they will rely on marketing skill and intuition, instead of technical expertise. They all have the same reaction I did. The attendees experience this revelation during the class because I designed the curriculum to focus on two primary needs of small business owners: saving time and saving cash. The SEO process you are about to learn is a practical, tactical, step-by-step road map. It is as efficient as it is effective.

During the most recent offering of this class, one of the participants, Cheri, asked me whether I had ever written a book on SEO. I told her no, but asked Cheri whether she thought I should. She exclaimed, "Yes, this is great stuff." That comment, combined with the overwhelmingly positive feedback I have received from clients whom I have consulted with at our Small Business Development Center, gave me the motivation I needed to write this book. My goal was to create something that provides small business owners with more than an entertaining or thought-provoking read. My goal was to deliver an educational tool that empowered business owners to become SEO experts, in much less time than it took me.

I will teach you how to implement my entire 15-step SEO process via easy-to-follow steps, which are then summarized into a checklist you can begin using immediately. The recommendations in this book represent a complete step-by-step SEO blueprint for your Web site. I am holding nothing back. Plus, the Quick Start Guide in Chapter 2 will give you a toolkit that consists of seven of the best — and totally free — SEO tools that I use every time I am optimizing a page of content.

I also produced a companion DVD for this book. The DVD is not required. However, if you struggle with any of the 15 steps in this process, and think you would benefit from actual demonstrations, then go to **www.SEOTrainingProducts.com** and buy the DVD. I realize I may sound like a self-promoter after I criticized some authors for the same thing. Here is the difference. The entire 15-step SEO process is explained within this book. The DVD provides demonstrations of the SEO tools, valuable FAQs from business owners, all during the actual Best Tactics for Online Marketing class I teach at the University of Wisconsin-La Crosse. The content on the DVD would be impossible to re-create in print.

If you are considering buying the DVD, I want to eliminate any risk by giving you a 110 percent money-back guarantee that ensures your results if you use the book and DVD together. This will hopefully give you confidence that what you are about to learn is a results-oriented, proven process. The details of the guarantee can be found in Chapter 2.

I divided the remainder of this briefing into four main topics: #1) why Google is the only search engine that matters, #2) key SEO terms you need to know, #3) calculating conversion rate with simple math, and #4) the most frequently asked questions (FAQs) that small business owners have asked me, either during one-on-one sessions on in class.

#1: Google — the Only Search Engine that Matters

Google's market share is staggering, and it continues to go up as more people defect from Yahoo! and MSN. According to figures from a comScore report published in May 2009, Google represents over 64 percent of all U.S.-based online searches. The findings within the report also showed that Google's market share increased during April 2009 while Yahoo! and MSN decreased. Yahoo!'s market share is reportedly 20.4 percent and MSN's is 8.2 percent.

Even Yahoo! essentially conceded its pay-per-click advertising revenue to Google when Yahoo! attempted to outsource this aspect of their operation to their top competitor in 2008. However, Google backed away from the deal when the United States government suggested there could be grounds for anti-trust proceedings. Google's rapid departure from the deal without any sign of legal posturing somewhat signified how unimportant the Yahoo! deal was to its overall business.

Given the decline of Yahoo!, and Google's market-share dominance in search, I specifically designed my 15-step SEO process to focus on Google. You will save time by optimizing your site according to what works with Google. Plus, your site will not only rank well in Google, but you will likely rank well in Yahoo! and MSN too. There are similarities in how Google, Yahoo!, and MSN index content and rank sites. Because of this, from an SEO perspective, Google is the only search engine that matters.

#2: Key SEO Terms You Need to Know

There are many SEO terms you could invest months in researching and studying, but nearly all of your time would be wasted. I have spent countless hours researching SEO, in both the private-sector and university, which has given me the ability to distill the unwieldy, confusing technical jargon into a small list of the terms that will provide you the most value. Every small business owner should understand the following:

1. **On-page and Off-page tactics:** On-page tactics include the specific steps you take to optimize the content within the confines of your site's pages. For example, bolding a keyword within a paragraph of content on your site is an example of an on-page tactic, or optimizing your page titles. Conversely, taking articles you have written and distributing them throughout the Web with the goal of increasing the number of inbound links to your site is an example of off-page tactics. The entire 15-step SEO process I developed uses a combination of on- and off-page tactics.

2. **Indexable:** The content of a Web page is considered indexable if the text (content) on a page can be highlighted by left-clicking your mouse and dragging it over the text. The text should be highlighted in blue, see Figure 1.1.

   Being able to highlight the text means that the text and any associated graphics on the page are essentially in different "layers," which is what Google needs because it can easily "index" the text-based content. Indexing is the process Google uses to scan a Web page for important details and then log them into their database for future keyword searching by Google users. Google cannot index text that is layered into a graphic or photo. However, Google can index the content it finds within Microsoft Word, PowerPoint, and PDF files you post on your site.

Figure 1.1

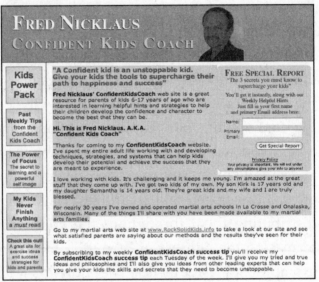

Adobe Flash®-based Web sites also create challenges for Google. In the past, Flash completely prevented Google from indexing content. I have read about Google and Adobe collaborating with the goal of making Flash-based content more indexable. However, I have not read any testing results regarding the success or failure of the experiment. Therefore, you will be best served by using text-based content and avoiding any design temptations to put your text content into Flash. I cover this in Chapter 3, when I discuss indexability in greater detail.

3. **Crawl, Spider, and Bot:** These are all catchy terms for the computer programs used by search engines to index your site's content. For example, Googlebot indexes a site's home page approximately every seven to ten days. Googlebot will come back and index an entire site approximately every 30 days. You can check the last time any Web page was indexed using the Google PageRank function within the Google Toolbar. The clock is ticking… make your site ready for Google's next visit.

4. **Page Title:** This is the first of several critical pieces of real estate within each of your Web site's individual content pages. The page title is the white text over the black background that appears in the upper left corner of your browser window. Both Internet Explorer and Mozilla Firefox display page titles in the same manner. Figure 1.2 is from the Home Page of **www.confidentkidscoach.com** and the page title reads "Confident Kids Coach – Confidence tips for kids. Fred Nicklaus' proven tips for building confidence in children – Mozilla Firefox."

Figure 1.2

Some Web designers/developers prefer to create a generic page title and then repeat it verbatim, or in some variation, throughout an entire Web site. This is a missed opportunity because the page title is the first place Google looks when indexing a site's content page to determine the page's relevance to the keywords found within the particular page's content.

A page's page title also becomes the clickable link that Google displays within its search results, as shown in Figure 1.3. For example, the clickable link for the No. 1-ranked site when searching on "Confident Kids Coach" in Google reads "Confident Kids Coach – Confidence tips for kids. Fred Nicklaus...," which is an exact match to the page title in Figure 1.2.

Figure 1.3

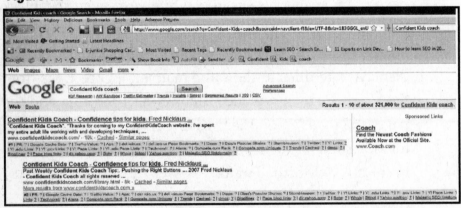

Because of this importance, in Chapter 5, I will teach you a step-by-step process for optimizing all your page titles so this valuable piece of real estate drives as much traffic as possible to your Web site.

For now, it is enough to know where page titles are displayed within a Web browser and how Google uses them to generate its search results.

5. **META Keywords and META Descriptions:** These fields are two more valuable pieces of real estate within each content page of your Web site. The META Keywords and META Description fields are found in your site's HTML source code. Do not worry if you are not familiar with viewing the source code. I will show you how to do it.

- Use your browser to open any content page within your Web site

- Use your mouse to click on the "View" menu to the right of the File and Edit menus in the upper left of your browser window

- Your browsers will then give you a drop-down menu with "Page Source" as one of the options. See Figure 1.4.

Figure 1.4

- Click on "Page Source" and a new window will appear that displays the page's HTML code within Notepad

- Or, if you are using Firefox as your browser, you can press the "Ctrl" and "U" keys simultaneously, and a source code window, like the one shown in Figure 1.5, will open for the Web page you are viewing.

For Figure 1.5, I opened the source code for **www. confidentkidscoach.com**. The META Keywords field is the first highlighted line in blue and reads: <META NAME="Keywords" CONTENT="fred nicklaus, martial arts american, karate, confidence, kids coach, coach, confident kids coach, kids health, healthy kids">

Figure 1.5

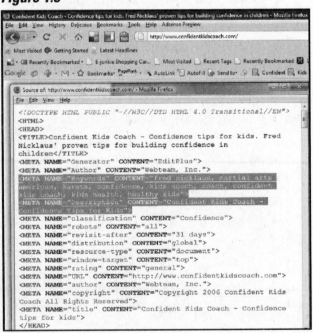

The META Description field is the second highlighted line in blue and reads: <META NAME= "Description" CONTENT= "Confident Kids Coach - Confidence Tips for Kids">

Googlebot loves both of these META fields. Although both of the META fields in these examples contain what seems to be good information, neither of the fields have been optimized. I will specifically show you how to optimize the META Keywords and META Description fields so they work in unison with your page titles to provide Google with the information it needs to properly index your Web site's content pages.

If you looked for the META Keywords and META Description fields on your Web pages and did not find them, do not worry. This is a common problem during the Web design process because developers tend to be focused on the design and usability of the site, and not necessarily content optimization. I will teach you how to easily fill in these holes during the optimization process. Or, if you want to fill in any holes right away, just go to **www.seotrainingproducts.com/tools** and copy-paste the code that is displayed on the page directly into your source code. You can then customize both META fields using the optimization process taught in Chapter 5 of this book.

6. **Keyword Prominence, Frequency, and Density:** all three of these terms deal with the location and repetition of the keywords you place within your page content. Keyword prominence is the determination of how close to the start of a sentence or paragraph a keyword appears. A keyword appearing at the top of the page, at the beginning of a sentence, and at the beginning of a paragraph will be considered more relevant by Google, versus keywords

found toward the bottom of the content.

Keyword frequency represents the number of times a given keyword or keyword phrase is repeated within the same page of content. For example, say you had a page of content on your site targeting the keyword phrase "endurance training," and within the content, the words "endurance training" were repeated 20 times. Your keyword frequency would be 20.

Keyword density takes your keyword frequency − 20 repetitions in this example − and divides it by the total number of words within the text-based content of the page. Let us say that the endurance training content page contains 500 words. If so, the keyword density score would be 4 percent, or 20 keyword repetitions divided by 500 total words of content ($20 \div 500 = .04$). With that said, keyword density has become much less important in recent years. Some of my colleagues within the SEO industry would even argue that keyword density is no longer a relevant measurement. Therefore, my 15-step SEO process does not focus on building your keyword density. I included this definition simply for your awareness, and so that if, at some point, you decided to work with an SEO service provider, and they began discussing their goal to build your keyword density, you could ask them to explain why that was an important measurement for the work they planned to do.

7. **Inbound Links:** are often referred to as "external links" and

are defined as links posted on other sites linking to your Web site. Figure 1.6 is a screen shot of the SEO X-ray tool. SEO X-ray can quickly calculate the number of inbound links to any Web page. Inbound links are extremely important because Google considers sites with more links to be more popular. Google could review two sites from the same industry with exactly the same content and optimization, and the site with the higher number of inbound links would be ranked higher because Google would consider the site to be more popular. I will show you exactly how to build the number of inbound links to your Web site during Step No. #15 of my SEO process.

Figure 1.6

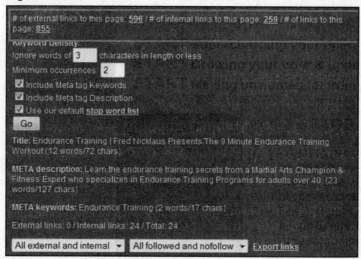

#3: Calculating Conversion Rate with Simple Math

In my opinion, conversion rate is the most important measurement you can use when evaluating the performance of your Web site. Conversion rate represents the revenue generated by your site and can be calculated with simple math. Conversion rate is the number of monthly orders divided by the number of monthly unique visitors to a site during the same period. "Unique visitors" represents all of the individual people or visitors who visited your Web site during a given month, no matter how many times they revisited your site during the same month. Each unique visitor only counts once, and that is what you want — to identify how many individual people are visiting your site.

The traffic statistics provided by your Web site host likely already include unique visitors. If not, begin using Google Analytics immediately. Google Analytics is free and provides unique visitor counts and other outstanding information. The Quick Start Guide I provide in Chapter 2 can walk you through creating your Google Analytics account.

Now, back to conversion rate. When you have identified your unique visitors for a given month, total up your online orders for the same month. Let us say your Web site generated 50 orders in January, and 2,000 unique visitors cruised through your site during the same time period. Your conversion rate would be 1 percent (20 orders ÷ 2,000 unique visitors = 1 percent). Or, restated, 1 percent of your unique visitors made a purchase.

You should also calculate your average order amount because you can combine this number with your conversion rate to develop some powerful "what if" scenarios. For example, let us say your 20 orders generated $1,500 in revenue, meaning your average order amount was $75 ($1,500 ÷ 20 orders = $75 average order).

Then, "what if" you increased your unique visitors from 2,000 to 4,000 per month while maintaining your conversion rate? This would result in doubling your monthly revenue (40 orders x $75 per order = $3,000). Or, what if you maintained your conversion rate while increasing prices? Consider how revenue and profit would change.

Here is another important reason to pay attention to conversion rate. The 1 percent used for the previous scenario is low. A typical rule of thumb to strive for is 2 to 4 percent. If your conversion rate is currently less than 2 percent, you should spend some time reviewing your site through the eyes of your customer. Are customers leaving your site before they complete their transaction — this is called "abandoned carts" — due to a difficult ordering process? Is your pricing too high? Is product selection too narrow or wide? Is product information difficult to find? All of these problems, and more, can negatively affect your Web site's conversion rate.

These statistics give you the power to be highly strategic. Calculating and tracking your Web site's conversion rate will make you quite familiar with what your site is delivering.

#4: Small Business Owner Frequently Asked Questions (FAQs)

I always encourage my class attendees to ask questions throughout a session and to not wait until the end. I love questions because I feel like they are a good way to break the ice, and, oddly enough, being asked questions helps me to relax and get into the class by interacting with everyone. Plus, the question-and-answer process is a fantastic peer-learning opportunity for all of the attendees because many people are struggling with the same issues.

When I taught the Best Tactics for Online Marketing class for the first time at the University of Wisconsin-La Crosse, I announced to the group: "I have time built into today's session for questions so please ask me whatever you like as we move along instead of waiting until the end." And then one person bravely raised their hand and asked a question, and I answered it. Well, whatever I said opened the proverbial question flood gate. Question after question was fired at me, and it was quite helpful. Attendees asked me about 60 questions over the course of nearly five action-packed hours.

I am going to use the final section of this chapter to share the Top 7 FAQs with you, just in case you might have similar questions. Chapter 8 also includes additional FAQs that you may find valuable.

Q: *Is investing my time toward SEO really worth it? What are some typical results that will benefit my site?*

   A: Excellent question, because if the results are insignificant, you would be better off investing your time and cash toward other areas of your business. If your site is not currently optimized, and you implement the 15-step process that I teach in this book, it is highly likely you will realize the following two primary benefits:

- Dramatically improved rankings in 30 days or less

- Doubling of your Web site's monthly unique visitors within 90 days or less

And, if you purchased the companion DVD to this book from **www.SEOTrainingProducts.com**, you already know that I will guarantee these results with my 110 percent money-back guarantee. How is that for an awesome return on investment?

I recommend that you take a baseline measurement of your current traffic statistics before you begin the optimization process so you can compare before and after results. Simply make a note of the month, day, and year you upload your first batch of optimized content pages/files so you can compare the number of monthly unique visitors before and after optimization. For example, if your Web site attracted 1,000 unique visitors in June 2009 before optimization, you will have this statistic available when you evaluate July's results using optimized content.

Q: *How much time does it take to optimize one page of* *content?*

A: It is important to recognize that you will not be as efficient in implementing the SEO process when you first begin as you will be once you have about ten pages under your belt. With that said, you will likely need to invest about one and a half to two hours per page of content that you decide to optimize as you build your familiarity with implementing the process.

However, once you move past the learning curve, you will be able to optimize a page of content in an hour or less. Plus, as you develop new content pages, optimization will simply become part of the process, and you will automatically begin writing pre-optimized content. You will no longer write content and then have to go back later to optimize it. Your experience with the process will remove the re-work and subsequent inefficiency.

Q : *My Web site contains about 40 content pages. Do I have to optimize all 40 pages?*

A: No, you do not have to optimize 100 percent of the pages within a Web site, and there are some pages you will never optimize due to their lack of content. For example, I do not recommend attempting to optimize miscellaneous, non-product-or-service-related pages, such as: Contact Us, About Us, and Privacy Policy. So, if your Web site consists of 40 product or services pages, I recommend starting with just 25 percent of the pages — 10 pages, in this case — as you begin your learning curve for this process.

This will likely take you anywhere between ten and 20 hours to complete, which is obviously a significant chunk of time. However, ten optimized pages are enough to provide you with some significant results. Plus, once you see what those ten optimized pages can do for you, I suspect you will be motivated to optimize your remaining pages, as well as add new pages. The key is to get started. The efficiencies will follow along with the results.

Q: How much time will I need to devote toward SEO every month, or can I just optimize the content and then forget about it?

A: SEO needs to be an ongoing process in order to generate the best results. For example, let us say you optimize a page of content, and then Google ranks it in the Top 10. If you are good enough to get into the Top 10, I suspect you could work your way into the Top 5. You may need to add another paragraph or two of optimized content to your Top 10 page. Or, you may need to build the number of inbound links to your Web site through additional partnerships or distributing articles. I cover all of this during Step 15 of the process, and it is not as complicated as it might initially seem.

To sum up, there are ongoing adjustments you can make to ensure your pages are ranked as high as possible, but there is obviously a trade-off between investing time into SEO and other aspects of your business. Perhaps a Top 10 ranking is good enough.

Q: At what point does it make sense for me to outsource the SEO work to an experienced vendor?

A: I recommend optimizing several pages yourself so that you can get over the learning curve of doing the work yourself. Plus, having this knowledge will make you a more informed consumer when or if you decide to meet with vendors. You will not feel intimidated if they start throwing terminology and processes around in an attempt to impress you.

I have developed some rules of thumb, or thresholds, for business owners to consider as they decide when to keep SEO in-house or when to outsource:

- Five to ten optimized pages will likely require about five to ten hours per month for you to manage properly, and can probably be done easily in-house.

- Ten to fifteen optimized pages will likely require about ten to fifteen hours per month to manage properly, so you may want to begin interviewing potential SEO vendors for future projects.

- 20 or more optimized pages will likely require about 20 hours per month to manage properly, so I recommend outsourcing at this level. You will have developed a significant amount of SEO experience at this point and will have become an educated consumer. Plus, off-loading 20 hours of monthly work to an experienced SEO vendor will be a boost to your personal productivity.

Q: How much do SEO vendors typically charge to optimize a small business Web site?

A: Prices tend to range from $500 to $1,500 per month for high-quality SEO work. The range is driven by the number of pages being managed each month, at a rate of about $75 to $100 per hour. Most SEO vendors will charge a set-up fee equal to approximately one month of the service plan you decide to contract. The vendor will likely optimize the selected pages during the setup process and then manage the pages throughout the remainder of the contract period. Plus, quality SEO vendors often perform some amount of link building work as part of their monthly fee.

Q: *Can investing time toward SEO boost my site traffic to the point where I can reduce my online advertising spending?*

A: Yes, SEO can have that benefit. When I was in the private sector, I consulted with a dot-com business owner who had increased his monthly gross revenues from an average of $10,000 to $100,000 per month within just 30 days when he decided to launch a Google AdWords campaign. I was stunned. However, the Google AdWords campaign was costing him about $2,000 per month. He wanted to see whether we could use SEO to help boost unique visitors to the point where he could reduce the amount he paid out to AdWords. I was able to score him several No. 1 rankings in Google, along with a bunch of Top 10 rankings. As a result, unique visitors increased. However, he never scaled back on the advertising spend because he was afraid of disrupting his revenue stream. I cannot say that I blame him. He had developed a highly profitable business model.

With that said, say your Web site is receiving, on average, about 5,000 unique visitors per month due to a Google AdWords campaign. Then you decide to implement SEO without making any adjustments to AdWords. Over the course of 90 days or so, you notice your unique visitors increase from 5,000 per month to 8,000 or even 10,000 per month. Theoretically, you could reduce your AdWords expense significantly, or perhaps eliminate it altogether, which would bring monthly visitors back to 5,000. However, I think most business owners in this situation would likely leave things alone and enjoy all the benefits of 10,000 unique visitors.

Your SEO Quick Start Guide

Your 110 Percent Guarantee

In addition to writing this book, I have created a practical, tactical companion DVD where I explain each of the 15 steps in the process via on-screen demonstrations, additional discussion, and some helpful examples. I created the DVD to supplement the book because the feedback that I have received in the classes I teach on campus is that having live visual aids is helpful to the learning process. This, unfortunately, is outside the realm of what can be accomplished in a printed book, making the DVD a valuable companion. The DVD is exclusively available for purchase at **www.SEOTrainingProducts.com** for $99.95.

As a comparison, when I teach the *Best Tactics for Online Marketing* class at the University of Wisconsin-La Crosse, the tuition cost is $89. One of the main upsides to the live class is that business owners and managers have the opportunity to ask me anything they want during the four to five hours we are together in the classroom. However, the downside is that once the class is over, some participants begin forgetting some of the topics we discussed, despite having their notes and the reference materials I provided during the session. Therefore, the DVD version of the 15-step process can serve as your permanent encapsulation of the class. The DVD can be studied repeatedly to help you develop an expertise in applying my SEO process.

There is a significant upside to purchasing the DVD and using it in conjunction with this book to optimize your Web site — the 110-percent guarantee I will place on your results when you use both the DVD and book. I guarantee you will experience the following amazing results if you use my 15-step process, as explained in the DVD and book, when optimizing your Web site:

1. **Dramatically improved rankings in 30 days or less:** For example, let us say your site is not currently ranked in Google, or if you are ranked, you are ranked No. 50 versus being ranked in the Top 10 for keywords relevant to your business and used by your customers. Research studies have shown that less than 1 percent of people click beyond the first page of search results — i.e., the Top 10. Implementing this 15-step process will dramatically improve your rankings, and you will likely score some Top 10s in Google along the way — all in 30 days or less.

2. **Doubling of your Web site's monthly unique visitors within 90 days or less:** Let us say your Web site is currently receiving 1,000 unique visitors a month. The tools and techniques within this 15-step process will deliver at least an additional 1,000 unique visitors per month within 90 days. Or, 2,000 unique visitors a month, as a result of the optimization. I am confident in making this guarantee because I have seen the results.

Not only do I guarantee your success, I am backing up my claims with a 110 percent guarantee. If you are not completely satisfied after 90 days of optimizing your Web site using all 15 steps in this process, I will refund 100 percent of your $99.95 purchase price when you return the DVD. I will even pay the $4.80 USPS priority mail flat rate fee to return the DVD. I will also provide you with an additional 10 percent bonus of $10, which would make your refund $114.75 ($99.95 for the DVD + your $10 bonus + $4.80 for shipping).

I have removed any risk to you by offering this 110 percent guarantee. I am obviously quite confident in your ability to produce amazing results when you use this 15-step SEO process. The process is time-tested and packed full of legitimate SEO tactics that Google loves. The process is also based on years of painstaking research.

Build Your Free SEO Toolkit

Developing a long list of possible keywords is often the first task small business owners begin working on in an attempt to optimize their Web site. Selecting awesome keywords is a crucial step; however, it is not the most important step. It is actually No. 4 in the 15-step process. For the time being, let us take a breather with respect to keywords and instead focus on building a free SEO toolkit.

Your Web site will be better served if you invest a few hours up front toward becoming familiar with the free SEO tools I have handpicked and organized for you. Several of the tools also offer paid versions. However, I have found the free versions to be robust enough and excellent sources of information, especially for no-nonsense small business owners who do not have time to wade through endless Web pages of data. I have eliminated the clutter for you and have prepared my concise, time-efficient list of seven recommendations. Plus, I will show you specifically how to use and/or install each tool.

One last important point before we get started: None of the Web sites or SEO tools I have recommended in this SEO Toolkit, or throughout the remainder of this book, have given me any compensation to do so. I am providing you with my completely unbiased opinions and recommendations based on my years of SEO experience and the use of a wide variety of online tools. With that said, let us review the SEO Toolkit:

1. Mozilla Firefox®

2. Google™ Toolbar

3. Google PageRank

4. Google Analytics

5. Google Webmaster Tools

6. Trellian Keyword Discovery Tool

7. SEO for Firefox

These are the top seven SEO tools that every small business owner needs to become familiar with using. Aside from being **free**, each of the tools has a short learning curve so you will be quickly up and running. The tools include an SEO-enhanced browser, research tools, and performance measurement. Some are fairly well know, like Mozilla Firefox or Google Analytics, so feel free to skip to the tools you are not familiar with and begin there to save additional time. Let us get started with Mozilla Firefox.

Mozilla Firefox®

Firefox is another Internet browser, like Microsoft's Internet Explorer. Go ahead and skip to No. 2 Google Toolbar if you are already using Firefox as your browser. I recommend using Firefox because of the SEO-related plug-ins that have been developed with the specific intent of helping people optimize their Web sites. Here are some quick instructions for downloading Firefox.

1). Open your Web browser and go to **www.mozilla.com**.

2). Click the green "Download Firefox – Free" button, as shown in Figure 2.1. This will begin the download process. Then, simply follow the on-screen prompts. You will be asked to make Firefox your default Web browser, and that is completely up to you. I actually prefer the usability of

Internet Explorer, so I continue to use it for my normal Web surfing. However, I rely on Firefox when I am optimizing because of the additional plug-ins. It is a matter of personal preference.

Google™ Toolbar

Figure 2.1

Google provides a number of terrific tools, and one of them is called the Google Toolbar. The toolbar essentially places several handy features and functions right at your fingertips, including a built-in Google search box and the Google PageRank tool (No. 3 in your toolbox). The 15-step SEO process is focused in achieving high rankings for your Web site in Google. The toolbar also includes the Google PageRank tool, which is next on the list.

Now, in case you have a strong preference for Yahoo! or another search engine, do not be concerned. If you optimize your Web site for Google, and rank well in Google, you will likely rank well in other search engines. Here are some quick, easy instructions for installing the Google Toolbar. Google Toolbar works for both Internet Explorer and Firefox.

1). Open your Web browser and go to **www.toolbar.google. com/.**

2). Click the blue "Download Google Toolbar" button on the right side of your screen.

Figure 2.2

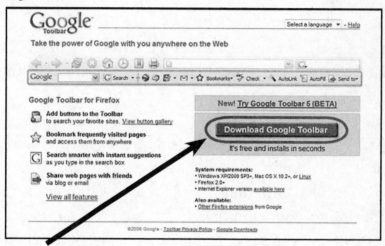

Google™ PageRank

It is time to begin using some of the wonderful features of the Google Toolbar – namely, Google™ PageRank. According to Google, "PageRank reflects our view of the importance of web pages by considering more than 500 million variables and two billion terms. Pages that we believe are important pages receive a higher PageRank and are more likely to appear at the top of the search results." PageRank essentially scores Web sites from a scale of one to ten, with ten being the most popular. PageRank is an interesting tool and a decent barometer of a site's popularity. However, I recommend looking at PageRank as one in a series of measures for performance and popularity. Let us now focus on activating PageRank inside the Google Toolbar.

Figure 2.3

Open a browser window and click on the green "Settings" button, located at the far right of your screen. After you click "Settings," a menu will appear with three choices; select "Options."

When you click "Options," a three-tabbed box like the one shown in Figure 2.4 will appear on your screen. The three tabs will be labeled "Features," "Buttons," and "More." Click on the "More" tab. The "More" tab will provide you with several categories of options that you can select. Some of them are extremely helpful features, so I encourage you to spend some time experimenting. However, since we are focused on PageRank right now, you will find its checkbox within the category of "Even More Buttons." Check the PageRank box. This will enable PageRank inside your Toolbar.

To see how PageRank works, open a Web browser window and visit any Web site. The PageRank score will be displayed, just like in Figure 2.5. The PageRank indicator is displayed next to the "Bookmarks" menu.

Figure 2.4

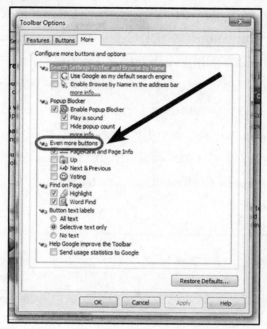

Figure 2.5

The PageRank of the Effective Behavior Web site is 3 out of 10. In my experience, you will likely achieve a score of 4 to 6 as a result of your optimization efforts. Please do not despair if your site is currently ranked less than 4 or over-delight if your site is ranked more than 6. There is always room for improvement, no matter what end of the spectrum your Web site currently inhabits.

Google™ Analytics

Google Analytics is a free service that has replaced the need for small business owners to invest any additional money toward high-quality traffic statistics in order to understand how their Web site is performing and which keywords are delivering the most traffic. Granted, if your Web site is hosted by a quality company, they likely provide some level of statistics as part of their package. However, Google Analytics tends to provide data that is more comprehensive, plus, it is fully integrated with Google AdWords, in case you ever decide to launch a pay-per-click advertising campaign to further boost your site traffic.

Figure 2.6

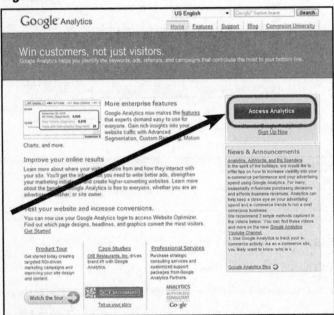

Figure 2.7

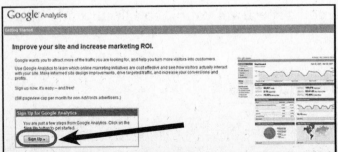

Click on the blue "Access Analytics" button from the Google Analytics Home Page. Or click the "Sign Up Now" link, if you do not have a Google account. Once you create an account with Google, you will be able to use the same username and password for Analytics, AdWords, Webmaster Tools, and a variety of other Google features.

Once signed in, you will be prompted to create a Google Analytics account. Click on the "Sign Up" button within the box titled "Sign up for Google Analytics." You will then be asked to enter some basic information about you and your Web site. This information is used to create your customized "Tracking Code."

Your customized Google Analytics Tracking Code will appear in a window that looks similar to the screenshot in Figure 2.8. Your next step is to copy and paste the tracking code into every page of your Web site that you want to have tracked. The code must be pasted immediately before the </body> tag.

Figure 2.8

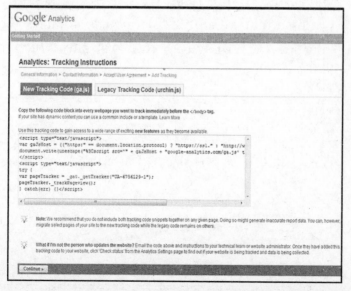

You can also open a Web browser and go to **www.google.com/support/googleanalytics/** if you have additional questions or concerns regarding how or where to paste the tracking code.

Google™ Webmaster Tools

Google also offers a variety of Webmaster tools, including the "site verification" function, which is helpful in letting Google know about new Web sites. All you need to do to get started is log into your Google account, where you will find "Webmaster Tools" listed under the "My Products" section. Click on "Webmaster Tools" and then enter your Web site's URL into the "Add Site" field. Click the "Add Site" button, and you will be taken through the verification process. You will be given two choices for verification methods: 1) add a META tag to your Web site, or 2) upload an HTML file. If you choose the META tag option, Google will then generate a custom META tag that you copy and paste into your Web site. Google will then visit your site to verify the code has been uploaded, which completes the verification process. The HTML file is slightly more involved, but essentially, Google asks you to create a Web page and post it at a specific URL within your Web site, which they will

Figure 2.9

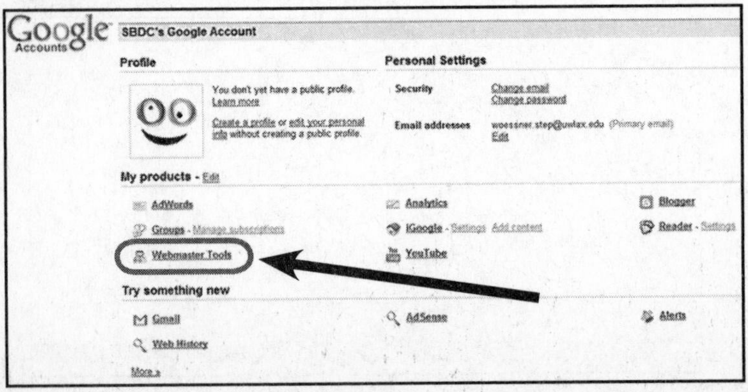

then visit to complete the verification process.

Verification is a wonderful way to get your Web site known to Google. You can also open a Web browser and go to **Google. com/support/webmasters/** to learn more about Google's site verification process.

Trellian Keyword Discovery Tool

While you likely already know the value of adding awesome keywords to your Web site, you also need to know how to determine which keywords to use. My 15-step SEO process will give you a simple, yet strategic process to help you select the best keywords.

Part of this process will be based on the data available through free keyword selection tools. One of my favorites is called the Keyword Discovery Tool by Trellian. You can access the tool by opening a Web browser and going to **www.keyworddiscovery. com/search.html**.

Figure 2.10

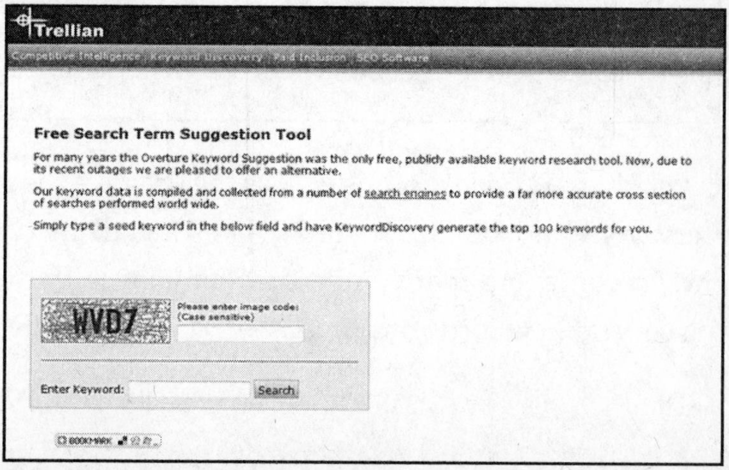

The Keyword Discovery Tool is highly user-friendly. You enter a keyword or phrase, and it provides a list of how often the keyword or phrase you entered was searched on within a given day. For example, say I was interested in the number of times the keyword/phrase "SEO Training" was used in searches. I enter the phrase, click the search button, and receive the data presented in Figure 2.11. The results tell me the phrase "SEO Training" is only used about nine times in any given day, which is not impressive. However, the Keyword Discovery Tool also provides results for similar or adjacent keywords that may not have been considered initially. Based on the results shown here, the phrase "SEO Training Course" looks like it would provide much better results, with 218 searches versus 9 for "SEO Training."

Figure 2.11

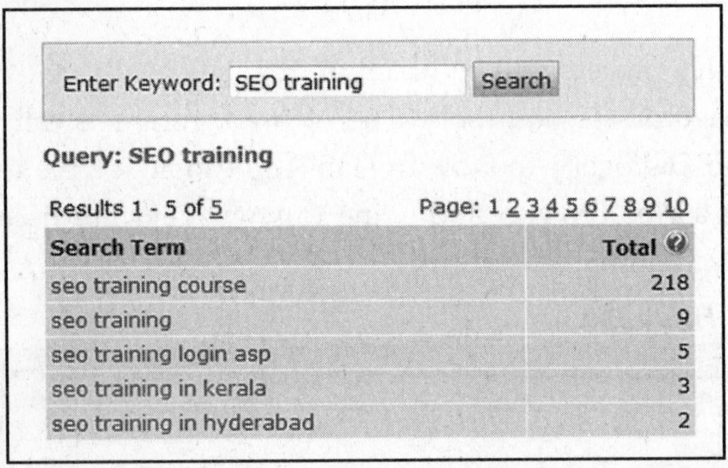

Enter Keyword: SEO training	Search

Query: SEO training

Results 1 - 5 of 5   Page: 1 2 3 4 5 6 7 8 9 10

Search Term	Total
seo training course	218
seo training	9
seo training login asp	5
seo training in kerala	3
seo training in hyderabad	2

I will cover keyword selection, as well as the usage of the Keyword Discovery Tool and others in step-by-step detail in Chapter 4. For now, I recommend that you become familiar with the tool by entering several keywords or phrases to view the results.

SEO for Firefox (SEO X-ray)

Aaron Wall of **www.SEOBook.com** has developed a number of free SEO tools, one of which is called SEO for Firefox. It is a good tool, but a little too complex for my preference. However, I like the SEO X-ray feature of the tool and highly recommend it as part of your SEO toolkit.

The X-ray feature will provide you with a quick on-screen snapshot of some helpful information, such as the content within the Page Title, META keywords, and META description fields for the specific Web page currently being viewed. SEO X-ray also calculates the number of external (inbound) links currently pointing back to the particular page you are currently viewing. This information is highlighted in red in Figure 2.12.

Figure 2.12

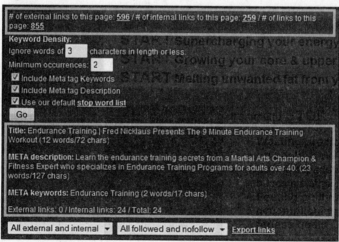

All this information can be found rather easily using techniques other than SEO X-ray, but what I like most about SEO X-ray is that it conveniently serves up helpful information in one easy-to-use screen or dashboard.

SEO for Firefox is an easy-to-install plug-in for your Firefox browser. You can read more about the SEO X-ray feature at **www. seobook.com/seo-firefox-now-seo-x-ray**.

SEO X-ray is easy to use. To activate the feature, right-click your mouse on whatever Web page is currently being viewed. Scroll down to the "SEO for Firefox" option on the menu and then select "SEO X-ray," as shown in Figure 2.13. Once selected, the on-screen snapshot of data will appear similar to Figure 2.12.

SEO X-ray also provides information regarding keyword density. I am not a particular fan of this statistic because I have not seen any relevant data supporting any claims that Google values it.

Figure 2.13

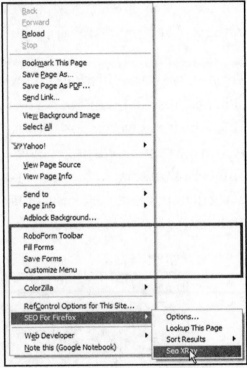

Immediate Actions Steps

You now have at your fingertips a powerful, 100 percent free SEO toolkit. There are a number of paid versions of the tools I covered, but in my experience, the free versions work well and provide the perfect amount of data for a small business owner. You will be best served by dedicating a little bit of time right now toward familiarizing yourself with the toolkit I assembled for you.

I prepared a quick checklist to help keep you on track. The checklist will likely take about two hours of your time to complete. It is important to complete the following checklist before proceeding with the 15 steps of my SEO process. Completing the checklist will ensure you are ready to hit the ground running and maximize your efficiency and effectiveness when implementing the process. Please make the checklist a top priority. The checklist will put you several steps closer to better rankings, more traffic, and more revenue.

A good friend once told me, "Fear and procrastination are the enemies of success." He could not have been more right.

Small Business Owner Optimization Checklist: Part 1

❏ Download and install the Mozilla Firefox browser

❏ Download and install the Google Toolbar and activate Google PageRank™

❏ Create a Google account

❏ Verify your Web site via Google's Webmaster Tools section

❏ Create a Google Analytics account and install tracking code into your Web site

❏ Begin experimenting with Trellian Keyword Discovery tool

❏ Visit **SEOBook.com** and install the SEO for Firefox plug-in (SEO X-ray)

❏ Proceed to Chapter 3: Become Google-friendly

Become Google-friendly

SEO steps covered in this chapter:

- Step 1: Verify indexability of Home Page and navigation
- Step 2: Add a site map

Let us get started with the 15-step process. The first two steps consist of making your Web site Google-friendly so Googlebot can effortlessly index all of your site's compelling content that you have invested so much time in developing.

Steps 1 and 2 are not difficult to implement, and if your Web site was designed within the last year or two, you may already have the first two steps completed. However, if some additional work is necessary, just remember that completing all 15 steps in unison forms a powerful marketing tool for your Web site that will pay huge dividends.

Step 1: Verify indexability of content and navigation

Earlier, I defined a Web page as indexable if the text on the page could be highlighted by left-clicking your mouse and dragging over the text. If you wanted to, you could "copy" and "paste" the text into a Word document. Being able to do this type of highlighting means the text and any associated graphics on the page are essentially in different "layers." Google wants the text and graphics to be separate because Googlebot can easily "index" the text-based content. Being able to highlight the text as I have described is the first test in determining the indexability of a Web page. The next test is determining whether Google is already indexing your Web site's pages properly. I will show you in the following four quick steps how you can verify whether Google has indexed a particular page within your Web site:

1.   Open any Web browser and visit your Web site.

2.   Click on the specific Web page that you want to verify for indexing. It can be any of your site's pages.

3.   Click the Google PageRank icon within your Google Toolbar — you should have enabled this during your review of the seven free tools I recommended within the SEO toolkit found in Chapter 2. When you click on the PageRank icon,

you will see a menu appear, similar to the one shown in Figure 3.1.

Figure 3.1

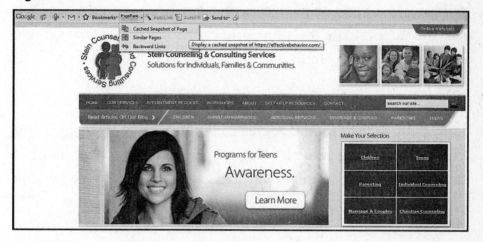

4. Then click on the "cached snapshot of page" option, and Google will confirm whether the page has been indexed.

For example, when you click "cached snapshot of page," a new header will appear above your Web page if Google has properly indexed your page. The header will look similar to the example shown in Figure 3.2. The header is only temporary and only appears in your browser. It does not affect what your Web page looks like for other visitors. The header includes some vital information, such as the day and time that Googlebot last indexed the Web page you are currently viewing.

Figure 3.2

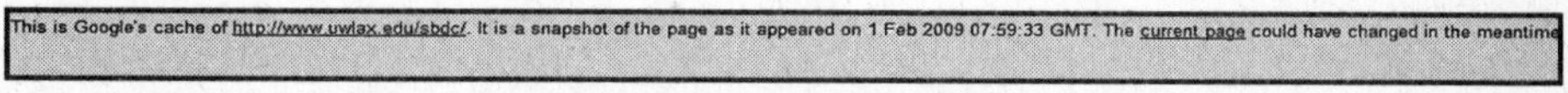

This is Google's cache of http://www.uwlax.edu/sbdc/. It is a snapshot of the page as it appeared on 1 Feb 2009 07:59:33 GMT. The current page could have changed in the meantime

Remember, Google will likely re-index your Web site's Home

Page every seven to ten days. Google will index your entire site approximately every 30 days.

You can repeat this same process for any page within your Web site. You can even use this process to check out the last time Google indexed your competitor's Web pages. The Internet is a level playing field.

Now, if for some reason Google has not indexed a Web page, you will see something similar to Figure 3.3. I created this screenshot using a brand new content page that I had recently created on the UW-La Crosse Web site in order to demonstrate what the results look like when Google has not indexed the page in question. Google wants to index every single page of content in your Web site, but they just want you to make it an efficient process for Googlebot.

Figure 3.3

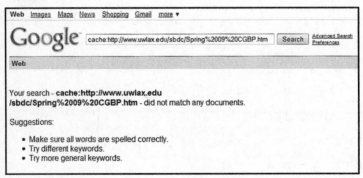

Let us say you too received a screen like this when you tested the indexability of your Web pages. This could mean several things: 1) the page is brand new and Google simply has not had enough time to come back and index the page, as with the UW-La

Crosse example I referenced, or 2) if the content page is not new and Google still has not indexed it, Google may be having a hard time finding it. The likely culprit is a broken link somewhere in your navigation that is supposed to link to the page. As soon as you clean up any linking issues, Googlebot will be able to cruise through your site and index all your content.

This serves as a good transition to the second part of Step 1. It is time to ensure that your site's navigation is also indexable along with the content. Just like your site's visitors, Googlebot follows your site's navigation like a road map to ensure successful indexing of every page of content within your site. However, if your navigation is not indexable, Googlebot essentially gets lost within your Web site and then either misses the pages or simply stops indexing your site altogether and leaves. Neither is a good scenario. You cannot visually judge the indexability of navigation because design has come a long way recently. It used to be that any navigation elements that were visually appealing involved the use of clickable images and, as a result, were not indexable by Google. However, that is not the case anymore. I do not think you have to compromise design for search engine friendliness.

There is a quick, easy way to test your navigation's indexability. Simply right-click your mouse on any navigation menu option and you will see a window open, like the one shown in Figure 3.4. I right-clicked on the "children" link. When I did, the menu box appeared. Now all you need to do is quickly scan the menu to see whether "Save Picture As" is available. If "Save Picture As" is not included in the menu, then your navigation is indexable.

However, if you are given the option of "Save Picture As" within

Figure 3.4

the menu, it means your site's navigation is image or graphic-based versus text-based. Google will not be able to properly index the graphic/image-based navigation and, consequently, may miss some of the valuable content within your Web site. Having a comprehensive XML-based Sitemap available for your Web site will help mitigate this risk. However, the best strategy is to use indexable navigation, along with an XML-based Sitemap. I cover the how-to's of creating an XML-based Sitemap during Step 2 of this chapter.

I would like to cover one more topic within the indexability subject, and that is using Adobe Flash® to produce Web site content. You may have visited Web sites that were produced entirely using Flash versus HTML. Aesthetically, a site created in Flash looks and functions beautifully. Flash-based sites can be highly attractive and functional for users. However, a Flash-based Web site creates significant obstacles for Google because Googlebot has real trouble indexing content that is embedded into Flash. Google wants and is primarily looking for text-based content; therefore, Flash creates an unnecessary roadblock for Google. You may have also visited Web sites that offer users the opportunity to select "HTML Site" or "Flash Site" from a Home/Landing Page. Although this satisfies Google's need for text-based content, it creates a content management burden by making the site owner/ web master essentially manage two different Web sites, which is an unnecessary hassle.

Just to be clear, I am a fan of Flash-based content. Flash video files (.flv) can be an outstanding addition to a Web site for product demonstrations, tutorials, and other applications. However, my recommendation is to embed the individual Flash files within an overall HTML site design. This type of integrated strategy gives Google the opportunity to still index your valuable text-based content and skip the Flash-based content, all the while proceeding efficiently through your Web site. Meanwhile, your human site visitors will still be impressed by the Flash-based content from a branding perspective. This is the perfect compromise between design, functionality, and search engine optimization.

Google's capability to index Flash-based content can be a hotly contested issue. You can visit Google's official Webmaster Central Blog at: **Googlewebmastercentral.blogspot.com** for detailed information on a wide variety of topics, including the indexing of Flash content.

Step 2: Add a Sitemap

In addition to indexable content and navigation, Google wants your Web site to include a sitemap. The value in creating a sitemap is that Google uses it as road map to help Googlebot find all of the content that you have invested valuable time and money toward creating. Theoretically, if your Web site's navigation is indexable and includes all of the content sections of your site, one could argue that you do not need a sitemap because Google is probably indexing most of your site content already. However, having a comprehensive sitemap will ensure that Google can easily index all your site content. Plus, if your content changes frequently, a sitemap will help ensure Google can quickly find all your latest content.

There are two different versions of sitemaps to consider. The lower-case "sitemap" refers to a static HTML page that simply lists all the content sections and sub-pages within your Web site.

Figure 3.5

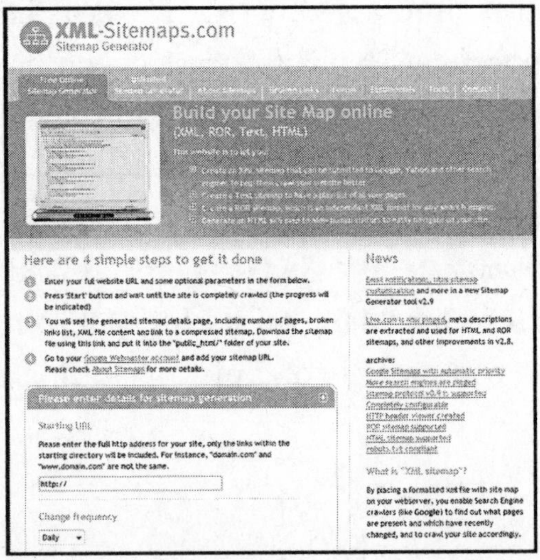

The upper case "Sitemap" is created using Extensible Markup Language (XML). A Sitemap is more sophisticated — but still easy to create — because it automatically lets Google know when content has been updated or when completely new content has been added. Because of these helpful features, a "Sitemap" is the best way to give Google the information it needs to efficiently index all the content within your Web site. According to Google, "a Sitemap is a list of the pages on your Web site. Creating and submitting a Sitemap helps ensure Google knows about all the pages on your site, including URLs that may not be discoverable by Google's normal crawling process."

Please do not worry if you are not familiar with how to create an XML-based Sitemap. I will show you specifically how to do it using a simple, free online tool called XML Site Maps Generator. The process to create an XML Sitemap only takes minutes to complete. Plus, I will also show you how to direct Google to where your XML Sitemap is located within your Web site so you can ensure all your content pages are indexed properly. Here is the process:

1. Go to **www.Xml-sitemaps.com**.

2. Enter your Web site's URL into the "Starting URL" field.

3. Fill in the additional information requested in the pull-down menus shown in Figure 3.6, i.e., "change frequency," "last modification," and "priority."

4. Then click on the "Start" button and wait until your Web site is completely crawled by the **XML-Sitemaps.com** tool.

Please note that only a Sitemap with a maximum of 500 pages can be created using the free version of this tool. There is a paid version of **XML-Sitemaps.com** if your Web site happens to exceed the 500-page limit. However, my guess is that this page limit will be just fine for most small business owners' Web sites.

Figure 3.6

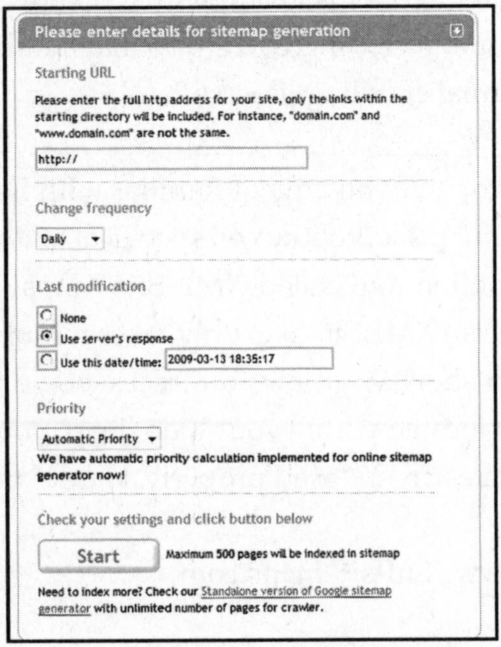

5. You will then see a generated Sitemap details page, including number of pages that have been included within your Sitemap, a list of any broken links that were found during the Sitemap creation process, and a link to the compressed Sitemap that has been prepared for you to download.

6. Click on the link provided and download your XML Sitemap file.

7. Upload the XML Sitemap file into the public_html/ folder of your Web site, and you have created your Sitemap.

You are now ready to let Google know where your Sitemap is located. To complete this simple process, you will need your username and password for the Google account you created as part of the Quick Start process explained in Chapter 2. Please stop here if you skipped this step in the Quick Start process, go to **www.google.com** to create your account, and follow the process in Chapter 2. Then log into your Google account and follow the next seven steps. These steps will also only take a few minutes to complete.

1. Go to **www.google.com**.

2. Click on "Sign In" in the upper right corner of your screen.

3. Enter your username and password and click the "Sign In" button.

4. Click on the "Webmaster Tools" link from the main menu.

5. Type your Web site domain name into the empty field that reads "click here to add a site" (shown in Figure 3.7) and then click the button "Add Site."

Figure 3.7

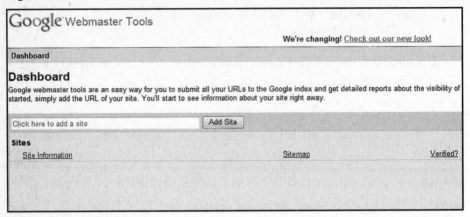

6. Once you click "Add Site," you should see a screen that looks similar to Figure 3.8, which simply confirms that the domain name you just entered has been added to your Google account.

7. The next step is to click on the "Verify your site" link, also shown in Figure 3.8.

Figure 3.8

8. Once you click on the link, you will receive a screen similar to what is shown in Figure 3.9.

Figure 3.9

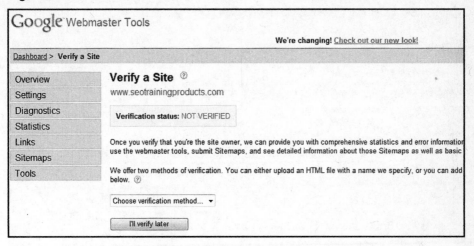

9. On this screen, you need to select the verification method you will use in order to enable Google to verify you are the site owner of the domain name you just added to your account. When you click the drop-down menu labeled "Choose verification method," you will receive two options: 1) add a meta tag, and 2) upload an HTML file. I have found the meta tag option to be the most efficient.

10. If you select the meta tag option, you should then receive a screen similar to Figure 3.10. With this option, Google will provide you with a unique meta tag for your domain name that you copy and paste into the first <head> section of your Home Page. Once you have inserted the code into your Home Page, click the "Verify" button on this Google Webmaster Tools page. Google will instantly visit your Web site to look for the code you just inserted. If Google finds the code, your site will become "verified" and added to Google for indexing. Google will also inform you if

Googlebot experienced any problems in verifying your site so you can make corrections.

Figure 3.10

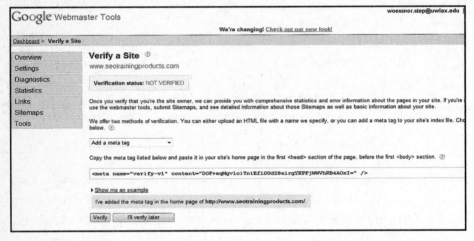

11. Once your Web site has been verified, it is time to tell Google where it can find the Sitemap you just created. Return to the main dashboard page shown in Figure 3.11 and click on the "Add" link found beneath the "Sitemap" link.

Figure 3.11

	Sitemap
Google Webmaster Tools	
We're changing! Check out our new look!	
Dashboard	
Dashboard	
Click here to add a site Add Site	
Sites	
Site Information	Sitemap
www.seotrainingproducts.com	Add
Delete Selected	
⬇ Download this table	

12. When you click "Add," you will be taken to a Google Web page where you can type in the URL of where your site map is located and click the "Submit Sitemap" button. See Figure 3.12.

Figure 3.12

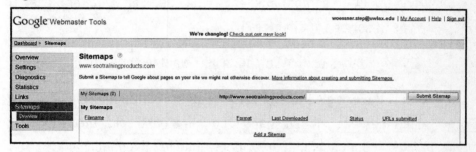

13. Google will immediately attempt to access your Sitemap to test the URL you just entered. You will receive an on-screen confirmation nearly instantaneously letting you know whether they were successful in locating your Sitemap.

Congratulations. You are finished with Steps 1 and 2 of my 15-step SEO process. You are well on your way to better rankings and more traffic. Now we will press on with the rest of the process and continue the momentum you have built.

Small Business Owner Optimization Checklist: Part 2

❑   Verify the indexability of your Web site by opening a Web browser and ensuring the Google Toolbar has been installed and the Google PageRank feature has been enabled (process was described in Chapter 2).

❑   Click on the specific Web page you want to verify for indexing.

❑   Click the Google PageRank icon within your Google Toolbar and then on "cached snapshot of page" to display the most recent day/time that Google indexed the page you are viewing.

❑   Now, create a Sitemap by going to **www.xml-sitemaps.com** and following the four simple steps on the XML-sitemaps Home Page.

❑   Upload your XML Sitemap file into the public_html/ folder of your Web site.

❑   Finally, inform Google of the location of your new XML Sitemap via Google's Webmaster Tool section.

❑   Proceed to Chapter 4: Strategic and Tactical Keyword Selection.

CHAPTER 4

Strategic and Tactical Keyword Selection

S EO step covered in this chapter:

- Step 3: Step-by-step blueprint to awesome keywords

It was a typical Monday morning on the University of Wisconsin-La Crosse campus until I received what I considered to be a special e-mail. The e-mail was an invitation to be one of several guest speakers to represent the University of Wisconsin at the Governor's Conference on Tourism. Tourism is a critical source of revenue and economic development in Wisconsin, and this annual conference is the premium trade show for thousands of tourism-related professionals in our state. And in 2009, La Crosse had been awarded the honor of hosting the event. Although I was thrilled to be invited to be a speaker at such a prestigious event, I am definitely not a tourism expert. My initial enthusiasm quickly turned to trepidation, until I took a few minutes to consider what I could offer that would be relevant to this group of tourism experts.

I began by assuming that it was likely that a high percentage of the tourism-related business owners and organizations in attendance would have Web sites. And, based on my experience, the majority of these Web sites would not be optimized. Every Web site needs more traffic, and every business owner wants to invest less money and time into their Web site. I now had a plan. My 15-step SEO process would be ideal for the conference attendees. However, my UW colleagues and I would also be under a serious time constraint because each roundtable discussion that we would be leading could only last 15 minutes. Then the conference attendees would rotate to another roundtable, and we would get a new group of professionals to teach. I could not possibly teach all 15 steps because that would take hours.

I thought about the overall SEO process and realized I could probably teach my keyword selection process in the allotted time, while still having plenty of time for questions and answers. However, this would seriously test my teaching skills, because I needed to succinctly explain the step-by-step keyword selection process in just one take. There would not be enough time to re-explain any details for people who did not completely understand it the first time around. Plus, there was another layer of complexity. I made the assumption the people who chose my roundtable would likely not have any prior knowledge of SEO terminology or any of the details I covered for you within Chapters 1 and 2 of this book.

Overall, I led five different roundtable sessions on search engine optimization. The people who attended the sessions were outstanding. Some even stayed after the 15-minute transition bell rang because they wanted to continue the discussion. They felt what we were discussing was that valuable to their business or organization. I think the conversations we had were exceptionally productive because the keyword selection process I use is so practical and tactical. Plus, the process does not require a person to have any technical skills in order to use it, other than being able to use a Web browser. It is also straightforward, so those who learn it can quickly envision themselves applying it at their first opportunity.

The One and Only Rule to Keyword Selection

I will show you how to select keywords that already have a proven track record of performance. To maximize your efficiency and effectiveness, the keywords you select must meet two criteria: 1) the keywords are realistic for you to score well with — they are not too competitive — and 2) the keywords have a track record for already being used by searchers. It is not until the time you find keywords that meet both of these criteria that you will begin investing time toward optimizing your site content. Having a disciplined, focused approach toward keyword selection will generate significant increases in Web site traffic when Google re-indexes your content pages.

There is also one rule I wrote that governs the overall keyword selection process. *The One and Only Rule: only select two keywords per content page.* I know this is likely contrary to much of what you have studied regarding search engine optimization. When I mention this rule to a business owner, or the participants in my campus classes, the reaction is often disbelief. However, the questionable looks always disappear once I offer up the following explanation.

You only need two keywords per page because Google, as well as your Web site's visitors, can only process and truly understand specific content pages. When a page covers too many topics, your visitors and Google will struggle at determining the most important theme on the given page. As a result, you lose the attention of your site's visitors and Google. Both will just move on to the next Web site.

Let us follow a more specific example from beginning to end in order to reinforce my rule. Say your Web site provides outdoor enthusiasts with information on the various types of activities someone might want to consider on a trip to the Black Hills of South Dakota. It would be a long list of activities, and it would be difficult to sufficiently write detailed explanations, let alone organize the content properly, within one long page. Visitors would much rather read a specific page devoted to each individual Black Hills activity, such as motorcycle byways, rock climbing, caving, and trout fishing. The only information a visitor receives if they click on the motorcycle page deals exclusively with riding throughout the Hills, nothing more. And then you provide links to your other specific content pages that might also be of interest to motorcycle enthusiasts.

Focusing your content pages as I have recommended will give you the ability to select just two keywords per page. You can easily incorporate two keywords into content, and throughout the other locations I recommend as part of this process, resulting in a focused, highly-optimized page of content. I will cover specific content pages in detail in Chapter 5. For now, it is sufficient to understand that selecting only two keywords per page of content will make your keyword selection process more efficient and effective. By following this rule, you will never waste your time incorporating a long list of keywords into your content. And once you have your list of specific keywords that have been proven to deliver results, I will show you how to specifically optimize your content step-by-step in Chapters 5 and 6.

Now on to the selection process, which is the exact same process I use every time I optimize a page of content on the UW-La Crosse Web site. I will teach you the entire process, and it will produce amazing results.

Collect Quality Data and Bet on Sure Things

You are about to be empowered to always wager your time investment on the keywords that will produce results, and you will accomplish this feat by implementing three simple sub-steps. These sub-steps will help you collect quantifiable decision-making data. I will explain how to execute each sub-step in detail.

Sub-steps within the Keyword Selection Process:

1. **Create your initial keyword list:** Develop a list of about ten keywords for each content page in your Web site that you plan to optimize.

2. **Download your free tracker:** Copy and paste your initial list of keywords to the free *Small Business Owner Keyword Tracker Worksheet* (I will give you instructions for downloading this valuable tool in just a bit).

3. **Collect data:** Use a free keyword tool and Google to collect two pieces of quantifiable data to validate the value of each suspected keyword.

Initial Keyword List

Earlier, I recommended that you optimize just 25 percent of your site's content pages as you begin your SEO learning curve and become familiar with the 15-step SEO process. Therefore, if this example fits your situation, you would develop an initial list of ten keywords for each of the ten pages, or a list of 100 initial keywords (10 keywords x 10 pages = 100 initial keywords). I recommend you develop an initial list of ten keywords per page so you have options to research and evaluate once you have the data available. If you want to begin the process with just five keywords per page, that is fine too. Indentifying fewer initial keywords reduces your options, but it also saves time, so it is simply a trade-off.

I recommend saving your keyword list in a Microsoft Word® or Excel® file or a similar type of document that permits copying and pasting.

Please note: "keyword" can refer to single words or to multi-word phrases — typically three or four words. The evaluation process I will show you shortly will be applied in the exact same manner, regardless of whether you are focusing on single words or multi-word phrases.

*** *Go ahead and take a break here. Try to spend about 15 minutes brainstorming and creating your initial list of keywords for the content pages you plan to optimize.* ***

Download Your Free Tracker

Now I will show you how to evaluate each of the keywords on your list using the Keyword Tracker Worksheet. Go to **www. SEOTrainingProducts.com/seotools** and you can download your free copy of *The Small Business Owner Keyword Tracker Worksheet* that I created for your use. The worksheet is an easy-to-use Microsoft Excel® (.xls) file that will help you keep track of and analyze the keyword data that I am about to teach you how to collect. I created an Excel 2003 and Excel 2007 version so you can download the appropriate file for your version of Microsoft Office®. Please open *Keyword Tracker Worksheet* once you have completed the download. The worksheet will look similar to what is shown in Figure 4.1.

Please find column A within the worksheet. It is labeled "Initial

Figure 4.1

	A	B	C	D	E	F	G
1	Small Business Owner Keyword Tracker Worksheet						
2							
3	Data Last Updated On: March 23, 2009						
4						"Exact Match" Search	Keyword
5	Initial Keywords	Google	Yahoo	MSN	Overall Daily Estimates	Google Indexed Pages	Targeting Ratio
6							
7	Enter Keyword 1	0	0	0	0	0	0.00
8	Enter Keyword 2	0	0	0	0	0	0.00
9	Enter Keyword 3	0	0	0	0	0	0.00
10	Enter Keyword 4	0	0	0	0	0	0.00
11	Enter Keyword 5	0	0	0	0	0	0.00
12	Enter Keyword 6	0	0	0	0	0	0.00
13	Enter Keyword 7	0	0	0	0	0	0.00
14	Enter Keyword 8	0	0	0	0	0	0.00
15	Enter Keyword 9	0	0	0	0	0	0.00
16	Enter Keyword 10	0	0	0	0	0	0.00

Keywords." Now copy your list of 100 initial keywords and paste them into column A. Following the copy-paste, your list of 100 keywords should run vertically from row 7 in the worksheet all the way to row 106.

Now that your initial keyword list has been imported, I will show you how to use columns B through G to complete your keyword selection process. Columns B through G will help you gather the quantifiable data. I will show you how to gather keyword usage data from Google, Yahoo, and MSN and divide it against the number of competitive pages already indexed within Google for the exact match of the keywords you are considering. This will result in what I call your *Keyword Targeting Ratio*. You will ultimately make your keyword selections based on the results displayed in column G.

Let us begin by collecting data for columns B, C, and D using my favorite keyword suggestion tool. This new tool can be found at **SEOBook.com** and was developed by Aaron Wall, one of the foremost SEO educators offering advice today. I prefer the **SEOBook.com** Keyword Suggestion Tool over the Trellian tool mentioned in Chapter 2 because the data it provides is a bit more sophisticated. For example, the data is segmented by the total number of daily searches across Google, Yahoo, and MSN. The Trellian tool provides you with similar data, but it is displayed as just one total number. The data provided by the Trellian tool is still valuable information, but I prefer to use it as a baseline and sometimes compare it against the **SEOBook.com** tool to see whether there are any discrepancies. Ultimately, my preference for the **SEOBook.com** tool is that it automatically segments the data by search engine. In order to determine the percentage of Google searches as part of the total searches identified in Trellian, you would need to take the results number and multiply it by .619 (Google's market share) to get an accurate estimate. I prefer to avoid this step to reduce time investment and boost efficiency.

The **SEOBook.com** Keyword Suggestion Tool is also my first choice because it provides search totals for the keyword specifically entered as well as similar keywords you might also want to consider during the selection process. You will likely encounter a number of instances when what you perceive to be a good keyword actually displays no results when searched using the tool. I will explain each of these points in more detail in the next section. In the meantime, you can find the **SEOBook.com** Keyword Suggestion Tool — shown in Figure 4.2 — at **http:// tools.seobook.com/keyword-tools/seobook**.

Figure 4.2

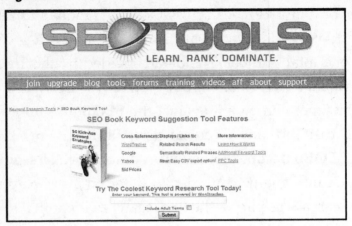

Data Collection

Now it is time for the somewhat tedious data collection portion of the keyword evaluation process. However, like anything else, practice will enable you to produce efficiencies, which will make the data collection process less time consuming as your experience increases. I have created a road map for you to follow so you can specifically measure and evaluate each of your 100 keywords using a combination of Google and **SEOBook.com** data. To get started, please do the following:

1. Open a Mozilla Firefox window and go to **www.Google. com**.

2. Open your copy of the *Keyword Tracker Worksheet*, which should contain your list of initial keywords, copied and pasted into the worksheet earlier.

3. Copy the first keyword in column A of your *Keyword Tracker Worksheet* and paste it into the Google search field.

4. Surround the keyword that you just pasted into the Google search field with quotes: "your keyword here." This will give you the ability to execute what is called an exact match search. For example, let us say you were interested in researching the value of endurance training as a keyword. Conducting an exact match search on "endurance training" tells Google that you only want to see the pages it has indexed relating specifically to the keyword you placed inside the quotes. The search result pages that Google displays for an exact match search will be your *direct competition* when trying to rank well for the keywords you are researching. Optimizing your content to rank well for exact match searches provides you with an outstanding benefit: visitors coming to your Web site after conducting an exact match search are likely more targeted, since they specifically searched for your type of content.

When a search is executed using a keyword without quotes, it is called a broad match. In this example, if you searched on endurance training without quotes, Google would display any of the pages it has indexed that relate to endurance training, endurance, and training. Because of this, broad match search results are not your competitors since, as the name implies, they are too broad.

We will only collect the number of indexed pages that result from exact-match searches for the purpose of evaluating the competitiveness of a keyword.

Ultimately, both searching types — exact and broad — are popular among Google users. Because of this, my SEO process will help you rank well for both types of searches so you do not miss any traffic-generating opportunities. I will cover all of the necessary steps in Chapter 6.

5. Click the Google Search button to display the number of exact-match indexed pages. Figure 4.3 is a continuation of the "endurance training" example mentioned earlier.

Figure 4.3

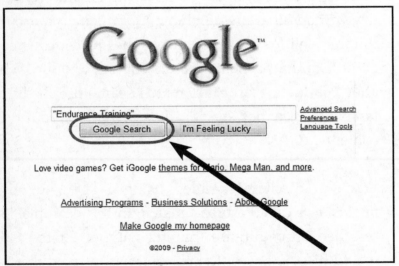

6. Now focus your attention on the upper right corner of the search results and you will see a line of text that reads "Results 1-10 of about...." Figure 4.4 shows the search results for the "endurance training" exact-match example.

Figure 4.4

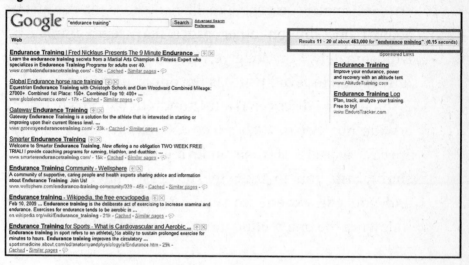

Again, the total number of results listed represents the number of index pages that will be your direct competition for the keyword you are currently evaluating via the exact match search. In this example, the total number of indexed pages in Google for "endurance training" is 463,000. On the surface, several hundred thousand indexed pages is seemingly a huge number, but do not get discouraged. You want to have a large number of competing pages because this tells you there is likely a market for the content with searches, since Google has indexed so much of it. On the flip side, if you had searched on "endurance training," and there were only 560 indexed pages listed, it is likely this keyword would have had zero to little value to you.

Here is a guideline to keep in mind that should boost your confidence as you evaluate the keywords on your list: You will have a good opportunity to score a high ranking for any keyword you choose, as long as the number of indexed pages in Google is less than one million when you conduct an exact-match search. I realize the idea of competing against one million other pages may seem unrealistic. Unfortunately, I cannot give you any specific reasons why one million indexed pages is the opportunity threshold. It is something I discovered after hundreds of hours in testing a wide number of Web pages. Google does not disclose specific aspects of their indexing process. Therefore, I simply ask you to trust the process I have developed, and you will experience superior results, just as I have, following the one million index pages guideline.

7. Now go ahead and type the total number of Google indexed pages into column F of the *Keyword Tracker Worksheet* for the keyword you are currently evaluating. Column F is labeled "Exact Match Google Indexed Pages." In continuing with the endurance training example, 486,000 should be entered into column F, as shown highlighted in Figure 4.5.

Figure 4.5

	A	B	C	D	E	F	G
1	Small Business Owner Keyword Tracker Worksheet						
2							
3	Data Last Updated On: March 23, 2009						
4						"Exact Match" Search	Keyword
5	Keyword	Google	Yahoo	MSN	Overall Daily Estimates	Google Indexed Pages	Targeting Ratio
6							
7	Endurance training	49	14	5	68	486,000	9,918.37
8	Enter Keyword 2	0	0	0	0	0	0.00
9	Enter Keyword 3	0	0	0	0	0	0.00
10	Enter Keyword 4	0	0	0	0	0	0.00
11	Enter Keyword 5	0	0	0	0	0	0.00
12	Enter Keyword 6	0	0	0	0	0	0.00
13	Enter Keyword 7	0	0	0	0	0	0.00
14	Enter Keyword 8	0	0	0	0	0	0.00
15	Enter Keyword 9	0	0	0	0	0	0.00
16	Enter Keyword 10	0	0	0	0	0	0.00

8. Now you would repeat this process for each of the keywords on your list in order to fill in column F of the

Keyword Tracker Worksheet.

The data in column F of your worksheet represents the first of two critical pieces of data you need in order to evaluate and measure the value of the initial keywords you selected. The second critical piece of data to collect will quantify the number of times the various keywords you are considering are searched on each day. The **SEOBook.com** Keyword Suggestion Tool will provide the necessary data. To get started, please do the following:

1. Open a Mozilla Firefox window, and go to **http://tools. seobook.com/keyword-tools/seobook/** to load the Keyword Suggestion Tool.

2. Open your copy of the *Keyword Tracker Worksheet*. Your worksheet should now contain your list of initial keywords that you copied and pasted into column A. In addition, your worksheet should also contain the corresponding number of Google's indexed pages for each keyword in column F.

3. Now copy the first keyword from column A of your worksheet and paste it into the open field in the **SEOBook. com** Keyword Suggestion Tool. Figure 4.6 continues with the endurance training example. It is not necessary to conduct an exact-match search using quotes, as you did when collecting the Google indexed pages data.

4. Now click the Submit button. Be sure to not press the Enter key on your keyboard, as this will not provide you with any results. You must click the Submit button.

Figure 4.6

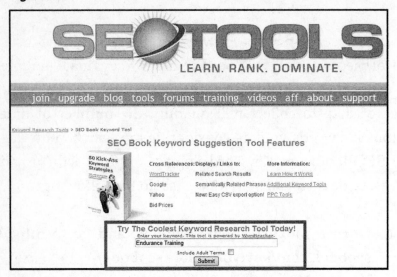

5. You should now see a list of results that show you an estimated number of times that endurance training is searched on each day using Google, Yahoo!, and MSN.

For the endurance training example, we can see that the keyword is searched an estimated 49 times in Google (72 percent market share), 14 times in Yahoo (20 percent market share), and 5 times in MSN (8 percent market share) for a daily total of 68 searches. Please see the highlighted red box in Figure 4.7.

The scenario I just described is based on the assumption the keyword you are currently evaluating is actively used on the Internet. I have entered many keywords into the Keyword Suggestion Tool, anticipating that the usage information would be outstanding, only to receive results of zero. This will likely happen to you a few times too, and please do not get discouraged. If it happens to you, just move on to the next keyword in your worksheet and continue the process.

Figure 4.7

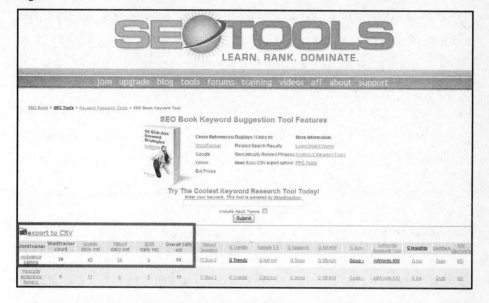

6. Now copy and paste the keyword usage data for each of your initial keywords into columns B, C, and D in your *Keyword Tracker Worksheet*.

Keyword Targeting Ratio

Congratulations on completing your work collecting the total number of Google's indexed pages and the daily usage estimates from the **SEOBook.com** Keyword Suggestion Tool for each of the keywords on your initial list. You should now have data entered into columns B through F in your *Keyword Tracker Worksheet* for each of your keywords, and when you entered all the data, a ratio for each keyword should have been automatically calculated for you and displayed within column G of your worksheet. I call this the **Keyword Targeting Ratio**.

The Keyword Targeting Ratio is calculated by dividing data from two columns in your worksheet. Let us break it down. The Keyword Targeting Ratio takes the number of indexed pages in Google (column F) for a specific keyword and divides it by the number of daily searches in Google (column B) for a specific keyword. Let us take a closer look at the endurance training example I referenced earlier. The Keyword Targeting Ratio for endurance training would be 9,919.37. Here is the math showing how the ratio was calculated:

486,000 indexed pages ÷ 49 daily searches in Google = 9,918.37

A ratio this high should be avoided. I recommend focusing on optimizing your content with keywords that produce a Keyword Targeting Ratio of 500 or less. Keywords with a ratio of 500 or less will provide you with the greatest value because they have an ideal blend of daily usage and a comparatively low number of indexed pages in Google that you will be competing against. This means you can score well for the keyword because it has less than one million indexed pages, and it would be worth your time investment because your customers and prospects are using the keyword frequently enough every day.

A Keyword Targeting Ratio of 500 provides you with an excellent opportunity to increase your Web site's traffic, and one of the goals of my SEO process is to help you double your site traffic within 90 days or less. It would be impossible to accomplish this goal by optimizing your content using keywords with ratios of more than 500. Keywords with ratios higher than 500 will not efficiently or effectively produce results for you.

A high ratio like that of the endurance training example indicates that the daily usage data for the keyword being analyzed is likely far too low. Plus, the total number of indexed pages in Google is likely too high. With that said, please be careful to avoid the mistake of targeting keywords that simply deliver high daily usage numbers. There are an infinite number of keywords that generate daily usage data into the thousands. However, these keywords will most likely fail the threshold of 1 million indexed pages in Google.

For example, if you entered the keyword "marketing" into the **SEOBook.com** Keyword Suggestion Tool, you would find that this keyword is searched on 2,310 times a day in Google (71 percent market share), or 3,259 total searches per day. Although that number sounds good, the keyword miserably fails the 1 million indexed pages threshold because Google currently has 688 million pages indexed for the keyword. This produces a whopping ratio of 297,835. Consequently, it would be nearly impossible to score a top 10 or better ranking in Google for "marketing." Plus, the keyword is so generic and vague that being ranked well for it would actually have little value.

Now, what should you do if several of the keywords you were evaluating for a particular page all have ratios that are less than 500? Quite frankly, this is an ideal situation. You can now be choosey. Simply select the two keywords from your list that would be the easiest to incorporate into the existing page content. No other steps are needed, and I will teach you in Chapters 5 and 6 how to specifically blend your keywords into your existing content.

To sum up the discussion about the Keyword Targeting Ratio: this simple number will increase your efficiency by giving you quality decision-making data from which to select proven keywords, saving you time. The Keyword Targeting Ratio also increases your effectiveness because you will only invest time toward optimizing content using keywords that are proven performers.

You will be well on your way to doubling your site's traffic if you target keywords with a ratio of 500 or less.

Figure 4.8

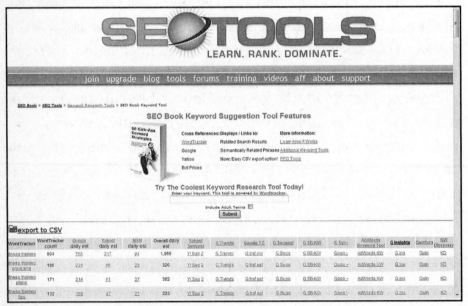

Similar Keywords

The previous section of this chapter provided you with a specific process to follow in order to select awesome keywords for your Web site. However, there is one more step that will further increase your efficiency and effectiveness, and you may have already noticed it when using the **SEOBook.com** Keyword Suggestion

Tool to collect data. The tool is so powerful that not only does it provide excellent daily usage information for the keyword you specifically entered, but it also gives you the usage data on what it considers to be similar keywords. This is such a valuable feature because it gives you the opportunity to evaluate additional keywords that you may have never considered. I also like this feature because the similar keywords sometimes prove to have more value than the one I originally decided to research.

I will illustrate the value of this feature with a quick example. Say your Web site has a page of content about fitness or wellness-related programs. The content you have written is educational and informative, but the page is not pulling in much traffic to your Web site. This seems odd because fitness is such a popular topic, so it seems realistic to assume there should be ample opportunities to attract people to your Web site. The lack of traffic could simply be caused by attempting to position your site to rank well for keywords that are too generic, broad, and uncompetitive — "fitness training" would be a perfect example.

If you enter "fitness training" into the **SEOBook.com** Keyword Suggestion Tool, you will see that it delivers a daily usage of 1,066, with 755 coming from Google users (71 percent market share). Figure 4.8 shows the results. However, an exact match search in Google for "fitness training" shows a total of 3,030,000 indexed pages. This produces a Keyword Targeting Ratio of 4,013. Again, we are looking for keywords that deliver a Keyword Targeting Ratio of 500 or less.

Therefore, I recommend you do not target "fitness training," or other keywords with similar data, primarily for two critical reasons: 1) the keyword is too broad, so it could represent anything related to fitness training, such as nutrition, clothing, gear, accessories, or programs. And 2) the top ranking sites in Google are well established, making it virtually impossible for you to develop a brand new page of content to score well against sites currently holding top positions for this keyword. I will now teach you how to apply the SEO X-ray tool from your SEO toolkit to determine which sites are well established in their current rankings, and which sites could be vulnerable to being out positioned by your SEO efforts.

The No. 1 ranked Web site in Google for fitness training is the Mayo Clinic, as seen in Figure 4.9. Realistically, your Web site is not going to oust the Mayo Clinic from its No. 1 position. The Mayo Clinic is a well-established, popular online destination. So let us take a closer look at the No. 2- and No. 3-ranked sites and use the SEO X-ray tool

Figure 4.9

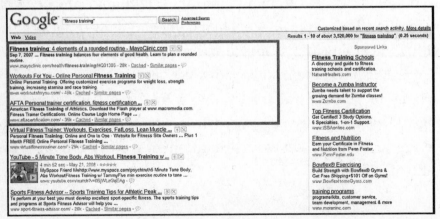

on both.

Click on the No. 2-ranked Web site, **www.workoutsforyou.com**. Once at the Web site's home page, I right-clicked my mouse and launched the SEO for Firefox tool. Remember, the SEO X-ray tool is only available when using Mozilla Firefox as your Web browser. Please refer back to the SEO toolkit instructions in Chapter 2 if you need a refresher on how to use this valuable tool.

Figure 4.10 was created using the SEO X-ray tool. It shows us that there are currently 5,240 external links pointing back to **www. workoutsforyou.com**. This is an impressive number, and one you will not be able to duplicate in a short period of time. It may take someone years of consistent SEO efforts to achieve similar results. The number of external links plays a significant role in your Google rankings. Essentially, the number of links to your Web

Figure 4.10

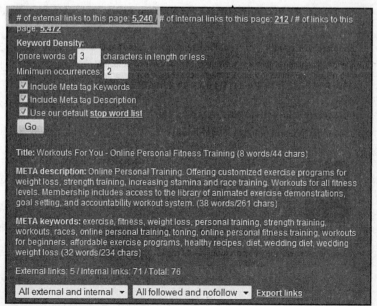

site gives Google a measure of the popularity of your Web site. Therefore, you not only want to optimize your content pages, but you want to boost the number of links back to your site in order to increase your rankings. I will cover this process in great detail in Chapter 7. Rest assured that link building is not a difficult process. However, it can become time consuming, and ultimately, our goal is increased efficiency and effectiveness with this SEO process, not developing a life-long commitment to certain keywords.

The No. 3-ranked Web site is **www.sport-fitness-advisor.com**, which has over 1,800 inbound links. To replicate 1,800 links may take you 12 months or more of diligent effort — again, too much time.

Therefore, based on the number of Google-indexed pages and the strength of several existing competitors, the keyword "fitness training" should be excluded from further consideration.

Now, let us go back and take a closer look at the **SEOBook.com** Keyword Suggestion Tool screen shot (Figure 4.11), and, more specifically, at the second keyword on the list: fitness training programs. This keyword is a perfect example of the similar, highly valuable keywords that the Keyword Suggestion Tool provides. "Fitness training programs" delivers a daily usage of 326, with 231 coming from Google users (71 percent market share). So far so good, but now, let us look at the indexed page data in Google. An exact-match search in Google for "fitness training programs" shows a total of 50,900 indexed pages. This produces a Keyword Targeting Ratio of 220 — outstanding.

Based on this data, I would definitely recommend the content page be adjusted to focus on "fitness training programs" as one of the two keywords targeted on the page. The second keyword would likely be one of the other similar keywords, also provided in the list from the Keyword Suggestion Tool.

Figure 4.11

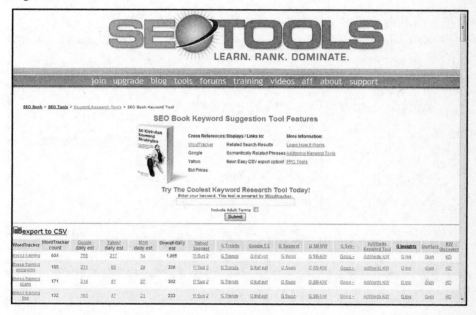

Small Business Owner Optimization Checklist: Part 3

❑ Develop an initial list of keywords for each content page you plan to optimize.

❑ Download your free *Small Business Owner Keyword Tracker Worksheet* from **www.SEOTrainingProducts.com/seotools**.

❑ Copy and paste your keyword list into the Keyword Tracker Worksheet.

❑ Complete the data collection process using Google and the **SEOBook.com** Keyword Suggestion Tool.

❑ Open a Mozilla Firefox window and go to **www.google.com**.

❑ Copy the first keyword in column A of your Keyword Tracker Worksheet and paste it into the **Google.com** search field.

❑ Surround the keyword with quotes, i.e., "your keyword here."

❑ Click the Google "Search" button to display the number of exact-match indexed pages.

❑ Type the total number of Google indexed pages into column F of the Keyword Tracker Worksheet for the keyword you are currently evaluating.

❑ Repeat this process for each of the keywords on your list.

❑ Open a Mozilla Firefox window and go to **http://tools.seobook.com/keyword-tools/seobook/** to load the Keyword Suggestion Tool.

Small Business Owner Optimization Checklist: Part 3 *(cont'd)*

❏ Copy the first keyword from column A of your Keyword Tracker Worksheet and paste it into the open field in the Keyword Suggestion Tool.

❏ Click the "Submit" button.

❏ Copy and paste the keyword usage data for each of your initial keywords into columns B, C, and D in your Keyword Tracker Worksheet.

❏ Evaluate the Keyword Targeting Ratio displayed in column G and exclude keywords with ratios that exceed 500.

❏ Evaluate similar keywords offered by the **SEOBook.com** Keyword Suggestion Tool and make final keyword selections.

❏ Proceed to Chapter 5: Optimize Your Site's Code.

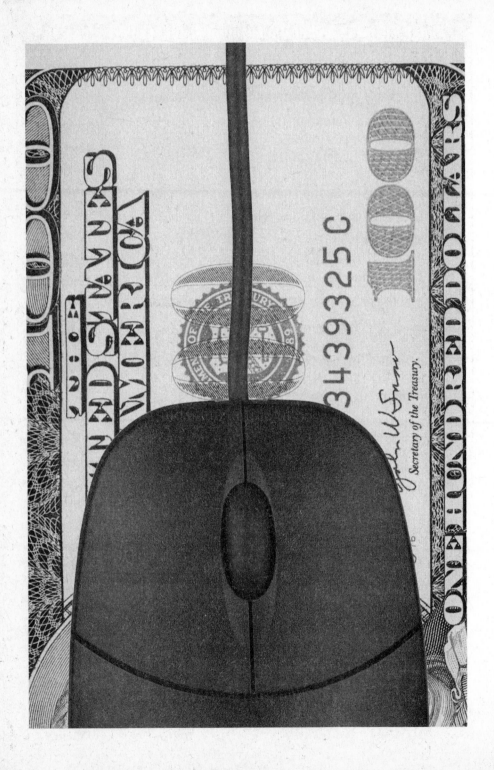

Optimize Your Site's Code

SEO steps covered in this chapter:

- Step 4: Create custom page titles
- Step 5: Create custom META keywords
- Step 6: Create custom META descriptions
- Step 7: Put <H> tags to work
- Step 8: Do not forget your URLs

You should now have a list of keywords that are proven performers based on what you learned in Chapter 4. You learned to use the tools and steps necessary for collecting quantifiable, measurable data and how to make good decisions based on the Keyword Targeting Ratio. The next step in the process will be to learn how to efficiently and effectively optimize your content pages for maximum results. This chapter begins that process.

Within steps 4, 5, and 6 of the SEO process, I will teach you how to optimize three of the most valuable pieces of real estate within your Web site: your page title, META keywords, and META descriptions. I will also show you how to put what are called "H-tags" to work for you and how to optimize the links to other pages within your Web site. The five steps covered in this chapter form the foundation of all the on-page optimization tactics you should implement throughout your Web site.

Step 4: Create Custom Page Titles

As you may recall from Chapter 1, the page title is the white text over the black background that appears in the upper left corner of your browser window. Both Internet Explorer and Mozilla Firefox display page titles in the same way. A page title is important because it is the first piece of information that tells your site visitors that they are in the correct place, i.e., that they found what they were searching for. A page title is also the first piece of data that Google collects about a content page. Plus, Google displays the page titles it collects as the links to the various Web sites in its search results.

To summarize, the page titles in your Web site play a significant role in your ability to increase your search engine rankings and site traffic, which is why you will need to develop a custom page title for every page in your Web site that you decide to optimize. There are no shortcuts here. A custom page title is critical to successfully increasing the ranking of your pages within Google and other search engines.

The good news is that optimizing your page titles is easy. You can be highly efficient and effective, especially if you invested time toward completing your Keyword Tracker Worksheet. To get started, open your Keyword Tracker Worksheet so you have access to your final list of keywords that you ultimately selected as a result of the process in Chapter 4.

Your next step is to identify the two keywords you plan to target for a particular page of content. To make this process more tangible, I am going to refer back to the example of the keyword "fitness training programs" used in Chapter 4, when I recommended selecting "fitness training programs" instead of the keyword "fitness training." The ratio for fitness training programs was just 220 versus 4,013 for fitness training. But this only gives us one keyword, and we need to select two keywords to target per page. The second keyword to target could be the next one on the list provided by the **SEOBook.com** Keyword Suggestion Tool, i.e., fitness training plans. In collecting some quick data from the Keyword Suggestion Tool and Google, I calculated a Keyword Targeting Ratio of just 31.68, which is perfect. Here is the math:

6,780 indexed pages ÷ 214 daily searches in Google = 31.68

So, if I owned a fitness-related Web site that included information on training programs or fitness routines, I would absolutely develop a page of content that focused on the keywords "fitness training programs" and "fitness training plans." These two keywords are highly compatible with one another and are searched on a total of 445 times a day in Google and the Keyword Targeting Ratios. They make an outstanding combination.

Now that we have our two keywords selected for this optimization example, we can use the following process to use them to create the perfectly optimized page title:

1. Open whatever version of HTML editing software you use to manage the content of your Web site, such as Microsoft SharePoint® or Adobe Dreamweaver®. You should be able to follow this process even if you built your Web site using online development tools provided by your hosting provider. These types of hosting + site development tools have become quite popular in the last several years. If you are using an online package, then just log into your Content Manager or Control Panel and navigate to the first page you want to optimize.

    If you are using SharePoint or Dreamweaver, you will be editing the actual HTML of your Web site in order to optimize your page titles. The HTML of your page title begins with <title>your current content here</title> and then ends. Figure 5.1 shows the page title from **www.combatendurancetraining.com**. To create this view, I went to **www.combatendurancetraining.com** and clicked the "View" menu followed by "Page Source."

Figure 5.1

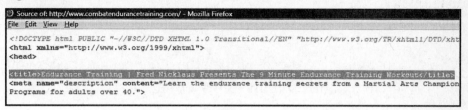

2. Open the HTML file for the content page you want to optimize.

3. Assuming you are using HTML editing software, simply highlight all of the content that is currently found within <title>current page title text</title> and delete it. Now you are ready to write your first custom page title.

4. Select the two keywords from your Keyword Tracking Worksheet that are most appropriate for the content page you want to optimize. Type them inside the title code, just like in this example: <title>Keyword 1 | Keyword 2</title>. To separate the keywords, I used what is called a pipe. The pipe is created by pressing the Shift key and the \ (backslash) key on your keyboard at the same time. In continuing with the fitness training program example, you would format the page title as <title>Fitness Training Programs | Fitness Training Plans</title>.

5. Finally, save the revised HTML file to your Web server in order to make the page title changes live on your Web site. Remember, Google will re-index this page in seven to ten days if you updated your Home Page, and within 30 days if you update any other content page within your Web site.

So within a short period of time, you should see an increase in your search engine rankings.

6. Now repeat the process for all the other content pages you plan to optimize within your Web site.

Step 5: Create custom META keywords

Now that you have learned how to optimize your page titles, I will show you how to optimize your META Keywords field, which I consider to be the second most valuable piece of real estate within your content pages. In Chapter 1, I showed you how you could view the source code of your Web pages in order to see your META Keywords. The META Keywords field is likely located in close proximity to the page title field that you just optimized. Optimizing your META Keywords field is remarkably easy, especially if you have just optimized your page titles. All you need to do is a simple copy-paste.

If for some reason your content pages do not currently contain the META Keywords field, do not worry. I will show you in a minute how to copy-paste the code from the Tools section of my Web site to fill in this important hole.

Let us now discuss properly optimizing your META Keywords field, which simply means making content consistent with the custom page title you just created for the same page of content. In order to optimize your META Keywords field, all you need to do is copy the content from the corresponding page title and paste it into the META keyword field. Just follow this process for optimum results:

1. Open the HTML editing software or online development tools that you used in optimizing your page title.

2. Open the HTML file for the content page you want to optimize.

3. Assuming you are using HTML editing software, simply highlight all the content currently found within quotes of the META Keywords field, as shown in this example: <meta name="keywords" content="keyword, another keyword, another keyword, another keyword, another keyword, another keyword, another keyword, another keyword, another keyword, another keyword, another keyword, another keyword, another keyword"/>.

4. Delete the content after you have highlighted it.

5. Now, copy the interior of the custom page title you previously created during the last section — i.e., <title>Fitness Training Programs | Fitness Training Plans</title> — and paste the content directly into the META Keywords field. Your optimized META Keywords field should now look like this: <meta name="keywords" content="Fitness Training Programs | Fitness Training Plans"/>.

6. Finally, save the revised HTML file to your Web server in order to make the META Keywords changes live on your

Web site.

7. Now repeat the process for all the other content pages you plan to optimize within your Web site.

8. If your content pages do not currently have the META Keywords field, just go to **www.seotrainingproducts.com/ seotools** and you can copy-paste the code that is displayed on the page directly into your source code. You can then customize the field using the process described above.

Step 6: Create custom META descriptions

Now let us take a closer look at the third most valuable piece of real estate within your content pages — the META Description. The META Description field is typically found in close proximity to your page title and the META Keywords field within the source code. Again, please go to **www.seotrainingproducts.com/seotools** and copy-paste the sample META Description I have provided into your source code if, for some reason, your content pages do not include META Descriptions.

Before I teach you how to optimize your META Descriptions, I want to briefly explain why I consider this field to be so valuable. In Chapter 1, I explained and demonstrated how Google uses your page titles to create the links that are displayed in the search results to users. Therefore, optimizing your page titles by including your two keywords for the particular content page not only increases your search engine rankings, but your prospects and customers see the keywords, which will likley increase your conversion rate, or the percentage of Google users who will click on your link versus another site. You get the double benefit of better rankings *and* more clicks.

Fortunately, Google uses your META Description field in a similar manner. In Figure 5.2, look at the text description that Google placed directly underneath the link to the Web site. The description reads: "At Active Trainer, you'll find hundreds of running, triathlon, cycling, walking, and strength and fitness training plans. In addition you can access Active…"

Figure 5.2

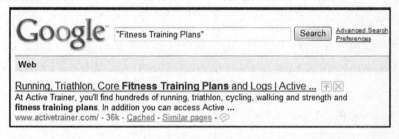

Remember, Google created the link to the Web site by using the content page's page title, and Google created the description by using the page's META Description. The description placed underneath the link gives Google searchers an idea of what type of content they can expect to find if they visit this Web site. Therefore, the optimization techniques that I am about to teach you to apply toward your META Description field will not only increase your search engine rankings, they should also increase the number of clicks you receive from Google users because your descriptions will include the keywords that were just searched.

I am going to show you how to optimize your META Description fields so that they not only appeal to Google searchers, but also help drive more clicks to your content pages. If you take the time to optimize your Page Titles and META Descriptions, you will not only increase your rankings for the keywords that your prospects and customers just searched, but you will likely increase your conversion rate of clicks to your Web site because your content will appear to be relevant, since it closely matches the keywords just searched.

There are only two guidelines to follow when creating a custom META Description:

1. Your custom META Description should only be 23 words in length. If your description is less than 23 words, it is a missed opportunity, as you could have said more about your content page to entice someone to click on your link. If you write a description that is more than 23 words, Google does not index the additional words. This is demonstrated by the example in Figure 5.2. By counting the words, you will see that Google has displayed 23 followed by an ellipse, meaning there is more to the description, but Google will not display it. Writing a description that is longer than 23 words does not provide you with value. In fact, more words dilutes what is called "keyword density," a term we will explore in this chapter.

2. Your custom META Description should use the two keywords for the corresponding content page at least twice within the 23 words. Again, refering back to the

example, we can see that the keyword "Fitness Training Plans" was only used once: "At Active Trainer, you'll find hundreds of running, triathlon, cycling, walking, and strength and **fitness training plans**. In addition you can access Active...." This is a missed opportunity to futher strengthen rankings. Using your keywords twice within your META Description builds your keyword frequency and keyword density. I defined these terms during Chapter 1, in case you would like to refer back to them.

Before I cover the META Description optimization process, let us refer back to Figure 5.2 to look at something important. Notice how Google **bolded** the keyword **"Fitness Training Plans"** within the link to the Web site (page title) as well as within the description displayed for Google searchers (META Description). By incorporating your keywords twice within your META Description, you will increase the number of **bolded words** that Google displays. The **bolding** visually tells Google searchers that your content page being ranked is more likely to have the content they need.

If you do not have the META Description field in your content pages, or if your fields are not optimized properly, Google compensates for this by pulling pieces of random content from the respective content page and then piecing together a description for you. However, the description sometimes is jumbled together and does not make any sense, not to mention that it is not optimized and provides the business owner will little value.

Now, for the META Description optimization process, just follow this process for optimum results:

1. Open the HTML editing software or online development tools that you used in optimizing your page title.

2. Open the HTML file for the content page you want to optimize.

3. Assuming you are using HTML editing software, simply highlight all the content that is currently found within quotes of the META Description field, as shown in this example: <meta name="description" content="delete this untargeted description and replace with something much better. A description that is 23 words or less and uses your keywords twice."/>.

4. Delete the content after you have highlighted it.

5. Now, write a custom META Description that follows the two guidelines explained earlier: 1) write 23 words or less, and 2) incorporate your keywords at least twice into the custom META description. For example, you should write something similar to this example: "Easy to follow fitness training programs! 14 different fitness training plans. Our fitness training plans provide a complete fitness training program that works!"

6. Your revised META Description, based on the example used in Step 5, would look like this: <meta name="description" content="Easy to follow fitness training programs! 14

different fitness training plans. Our fitness training plans provide a complete fitness training program that works!" />.

7. Finally, save the revised HTML file to your Web server in order to make the META Description changes live on your Web site.

8. Now repeat the process for all the other content pages you plan to optimize within your Web site.

I would like to quickly organize and recap the formatting of these three important pieces of real estate within your Web site before we move into Step 7 of the overall 15-step SEO process. I will use the Fitness Training Programs and Fitness Training Plans keywords introduce earlier to help illustrate this example. Follow the principles of these examples when you optimize your content pages, and you will be pleased with the return on your time investment.

Example of an Optimized Page Title

<title>Fitness Training Programs | Fitness Training Plans</title>

Example of an Optimized META Keywords field

<meta name="keywords" content="Fitness Training Programs | Fitness Training Plans" />

Example of an Optimized META Description field

<meta name="description" content="Easy to follow fitness

training programs! 14 different fitness training plans. Our fitness training plans provide a complete fitness training program that works!" />

Step 7: Put headings to work

It is highly likely that each content page within your Web site already includes features called headings, which are also referred to as H-tags. Headings are essentially used to form the titles of paragraphs or to emphasize certain content sections on a page that you want to highlight to your site visitors by using a larger and/or bold font, similar to when you choose to use a heading within a Microsoft Word® document. And headings also appeal to Google in the same way. Headings tell Google that this content is important and needs to be given special attention.

Aaron Wall, owner of **SEOBook.com**, has published an outstanding glossary of SEO terms, which has been included at the end of this book. The glossary also defines headings, and I have included that definition here for easy reference. "The heading element briefly describes the subject of the section it introduces. Heading elements go from H1 to H6 with the lower numbered headings being most important. You should only use a single H1 element on each page, and may want to use multiple other heading elements to structure a document. An H1 element source would look like: <h1>Your Topic</h1>." You can look up other SEO-related terms in the full **SEOBook.com** glossary, reprinted with Aaron's permission at the back of this book for reference.

In Figure 5.3, a screenshot taken from **www.effectivebehavior.**

com/category/christian-marriages/, the headline that reads "Increasing Intimacy – What the Research Says" is one of the several headers — or H-tags — that can be found on this page. We will review each of the headers that make up this page shortly.

Figure 5.3

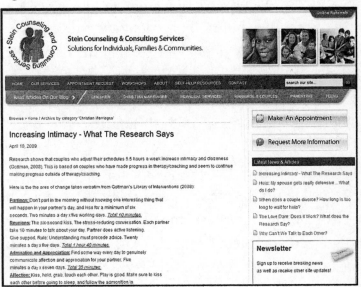

If your Web site was developed using custom HTML, it will be easy for you to optimize your headings. However, even though your site was developed in HTML, this is not a guarantee that headings currently exist. Even if you have headlines in your content, this does not necessarily mean that the headline is an actual H-tag. For example, I recently met with a client at the UW-La Crosse Small Business Development Center to review her Web site and discuss how she could use SEO to boost her search engine rankings. We focused our discussion toward one particular content page so she could see how the 15-step SEO process should be applied. She would then be able to follow the process and apply the steps on the subsequent content pages throughout her Web site. This particular business owner has some excellent content pages and works with a freelance Web designer who seemingly does good work. At first glance, I thought the content page our client selected to discuss seemed to be in a decent format. There was a headline at the top of the page followed by several paragraphs of text and photos — nothing remarkable, but nothing blatantly out of place either. I reviewed the source code and could see that the Page Title, META Keywords, and META Description fields had yet to be optimized. In addition, I used the **SEOBook.com** SEO X-ray tool — as discussed in Chapter 2 — to highlight all of the headings on the page.

To my amazement, the SEO X-ray tool showed that even though this business owner's content page included a nice headline positioned at the top of the page, the Web developer had not placed the headline content into a formal H1 tag. I assured the business owner that this is easy to correct, and I will teach you how to it do as well in case you happen to be in the same situation.

I shared this short story with you so that you do not take anything for granted. Even if your site was created by a Web development professional, some things may have been missed. Ultimately, you as the business owner need to double check to ensure that your site has every opportunity to create the results you expect. I am going to teach you how to fill in any holes you might uncover during your review.

Finally, as a completely different scenario, let us say you developed your Web site using an online content management system instead of custom HTML. Most content management systems should provide the opportunity to add, and therefore optimize, the headings within a content page.

Let us begin the optimization process with some quick how-to instructions for viewing the headings within a particular content page of your Web site. I will demonstrate the process by viewing the same content page from **www.effectivebehavior.com** through the eyes of the SEO X-ray tool. I think this tool is extremely valuable because it efficiently and effectively highlights all the H-tags used throughout a content page and displays them visually for you in an easy-to-understand format. Figure 5.4 illustrates the process I used for highlighting the H-tags for the **www.effectivebehavior. com** content page.

Figure 5.4

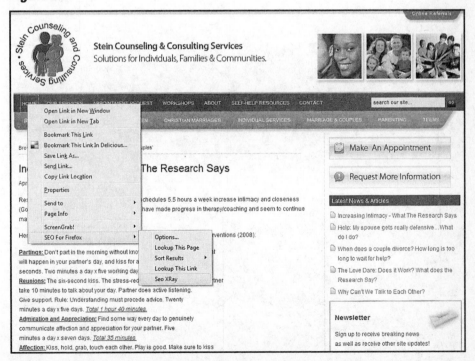

1. Open a Firefox browser window and go to the content page within your Web site that you want to test. For this example, I went to **www.effectivebehavior.com/category/ christian-marriages/**.

2. Right-click your mouse to activate the on-screen SEO for Firefox menu.

3. Click on "SEO for Firefox," located at the bottom of the menu. This will open a sub-menu with the option of "SEO X-ray" at the bottom of the sub-menu.

4. Click on "SEO X-ray." This will launch the SEO X-ray tool and display the headers found within the content page. See Figure 5.5 for the results of this example.

Figure 5.5

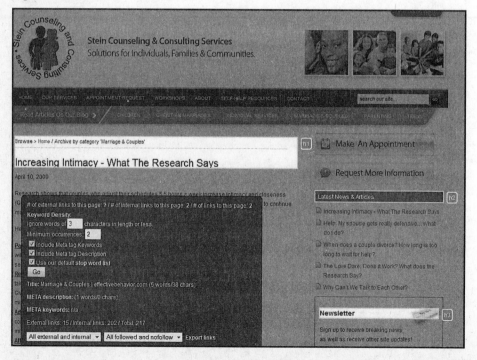

As you can see in Figure 5.5, this content page actually consists of three headings of H-tags. The headline "Increasing Intimacy – What the Research Says" is formatted as an H1-tag, followed by "Latest News & Articles" as an H2-tag, and "Newsletter" as an H3-tag.

For some content pages, it may make sense to optimize all the H-tags. Or, as in the case of the **Effectivebehavior.com** content page we are looking at, there is only value in optimizing the H1-tag on this page because the same H2- and H3-tags are actually repeated throughout every content page within the Web site, which would make it impossible to optimize for the "Increasing Intimacy – What the Research Says" content page. You may encounter a similar situation within your own Web site. Optimizing your H1 tag is the main priority. If your content page includes additional H-tags, this is an added bonus.

Now for the H-tag optimization process. Just follow this process for optimum results:

1. Open the HTML editing software or online development tools that you have used during the earlier steps of the optimization process.

2. Open the HTML file for the content page you want to optimize.

3. Assuming you are using HTML editing software, simply highlight all the content that is currently found within the H1 tag field, as shown in this example: <h1> headline that

needs to be optimized</h1>

4. Delete the content after you have highlighted it.

5. Now, copy the interior of the custom page title you previously created for this page during the last section — i.e., <title>Fitness Training Programs | Fitness Training Plans</title> — and paste the content directly into the H1-tag field. Your optimized H1-tag field should now look like this: <h1>Fitness Training Programs | Fitness Training Plans</h1>.

6. The final change is to delete the pipe (|) that is currently separating the two keywords and replace it with a hyphen (-) for the H-tag. Therefore, the final version of your optimized H1-tag should look like this: <h1>Fitness Training Programs - Fitness Training Plans</h1>.

7. Finally, save the revised HTML file to your Web server in order to make the H1-tag change live on your Web site.

8. Now repeat the process for all the other content pages you plan to optimize within your Web site.

Now, if you have a headline on your content page, but it is not formatted as an H1-tag — similar to the business owner I met with recently — Simply follow this process:

1. Open the HTML editing software or online development tools that you have used during the earlier steps of the

optimization process.

2. Open the HTML file for the content page you want to optimize.

3. Assuming you are using HTML editing software, find the current version of the headline and add the beginning and ending H1-tagging to the headline. For example, you will need to type <h1> immediately before the headline and </h1> immediately following the headline. Your H1-tag field should now look like this example: <h1> headline that needs to be optimized</h1>. Now follow the remainder of the H1-tag optimization process.

4. Assuming you are using HTML editing software, simply highlight all the content that is currently found within the H1 tag field, as shown in this example: <h1>headline that needs to be optimized</h1>.

5. Delete the content after you have highlighted it.

6. Now, copy the interior of the custom page title you previously created for this page during the last section — i.e., <title>Fitness Training Programs | Fitness Training Plans</title> — and paste the content directly into the H1-tag field. Your optimized H1-tag field should now look like this: <h1>Fitness Training Programs | Fitness Training Plans</h1>.

7. The final change is to delete the pipe (|) that is currently

separating the two keywords and replace it with a hyphen (-) for the H-tag. Therefore, the final version of your optimized H1-tag should look like this: <h1>Fitness Training Programs - Fitness Training Plans</h1>.

8. Finally, save the revised HTML file to your Web server in order to make the H1-tag change live on your Web site.

9. Now repeat the process for all the other content pages you plan to optimize within your Web site.

Step 8: Do not forget your URLs

You are now nearly 50 percent of the way through my 15-step SEO process. I hope you have found it to be efficient and easier to implement than perhaps you had anticipated when you began studying this book.

Step 8 will focus on the Uniform Resource Locators (URLs) of the content pages you plan to optimize throughout your Web site. Just for clarification, there are two terms here that are important to not get confused. The first is **domain name**. Your domain name is the first part of your Web site address, and it often serves as the URL for your Home Page. For example, for my Web site, **SEOTrainingProducts.com** is my domain name. The domain name is also used in the corresponding e-mail address, such as info@seotrainingproducts.com.

The second term is **URL**. During Step 4 of the SEO process, I recommended that you visit **SEOTrainingProducts.com/seotools** to download your free copy of the Small Business Owner Keyword Tracker Worksheet. The Web site address **SEOTrainingProducts. com/seotools** is the URL, or location, where a person can find the content page in order to download the free Excel worksheet. URLs are not used in e-mail addresses.

The good thing about domain names and URLs is that you can place keywords inside of both. Google reviews your domain name and the full URL for the content page during its indexing process. Let us look at my Web site domain name again as the first example: **SEOTrainingProducts.com**. My domain name consists of four different keyword combinations that Google users could potentially use during searches. I have bolded and underlined the four possible combinations here for your review:

- <u>**SEO**</u>TrainingProducts.com
- <u>**SEOTraining**</u>Products.com
- <u>**SEOTrainingProducts**</u>.com
- <u>**SEO**</u>Training<u>**Products**</u>.com

Therefore, when you select a domain name, especially for a new business or Web site, I recommend you consider what your prospective customers and Google users may search for in the future, and then develop a domain name that incorporates the keyword(s).

Most business owners I have consulted with have a strong preference to register the name of their company as their domain name. And for an established business, that makes complete sense, given the likelihood that the company's name is well recognized and the business has a good reputation. Plus, there are some searchers who just try and guess at the domain name for a business by typing in the company's name and adding a ".com" at the end, versus using Google to conduct a search. For those types of customers, using the company name as the domain name is a good strategy.

For the moment, I will assume that you already have an existing Web site and that you used your business name as the domain name. There are still some significant optimization opportunities that you can take advantage of, and those opportunities come in the form of optimizing the content page URLs for the specific content pages you are optimizing within your Web site.

For example, during the indexing process, Google is looking for matches between your Page Title, META Keywords, META Description, domain name, full URL, and the content on the actual page. Adding keywords into your URL will create an additional match for your Web site. For example, look at Figure 5.6, a screenshot I created after conducting an exact-match search in Google for the keywords "Chrysler Town and County."

The No. 1-ranked content page in the search results included the specific words "Chrysler Town and Country" within the page title, which was one of the primary reasons it was ranked in the top position. However, look at the content page ranked No. 3. The link (Page Title) reads: Chrysler Town & Country Review – Edmunds.com. I suspect there are two main reasons why the No. 3-ranked content page was not ranked #1 by Google: 1) the No. 1-ranked site had the word "Chrysler" in the domain name, and 2)

Figure 5.6

the No. 3-ranked site used "&" in the Page Title instead of "and" to separate the words "Town" and "Country."

I found this to be ironic, because the META Description was formatted properly and could have provided additional consistency with the Page Title. However, there is also another important observation with the No. 3-ranked Web site. Look closely at the URL, which is positioned under the META Description. Notice how Google placed the words **Chrysler/townandcountry** all in bold. The bolding is visually demonstrating how Google found consistencies between the content page's META Description and the URL. Now, had this Web site also formatted the Page Title using the word "and" instead of "&," there would have been bolding in three different locations.

It is unlikely this page would have displaced Chrysler from the No. 1 position, but most small business owners will not be competing against Chrysler — meaning if you optimize your Page Title, META Keywords, META Description, domain name, full URL, and the content on the actual page, Google will reward you with good rankings.

I will explain the steps you need to take to optimize your URLs to achieve optimal results, but first, a word of caution. If Google has already indexed your Web site, then by going back through and optimizing your URLs, you will essentially be creating brand new pages according to Google, because the pages that are currently indexed will no longer exist in their previous locations. They will have different URLs. Therefore, I recommend you proceed with caution and only optimize the URLs of a few pages per month. And update your Sitemap immediately so that Google can find the new URL as efficiently as possible.

Now, here is the optimization process you need to use:

1. Open the HTML editing software or online development tools that you have used during the earlier steps of the optimization process.

2. Within the software, there should be an option for you to type in whatever you want to specify as the URL. I use Microsoft SharePoint® as my primary HTML editor on campus. To follow is the series of steps I used when I optimized the URL for the CGBP content page on the UW-La Crosse Web site using SharePoint.

   a. Step 1: open the HTML file for the content page you want to optimize by clicking on the page's current URL from the list of URLs displayed on the left side of your screen. See Figure 5.7. Once selected, the content page will be made available to you for editing.

Figure 5.7

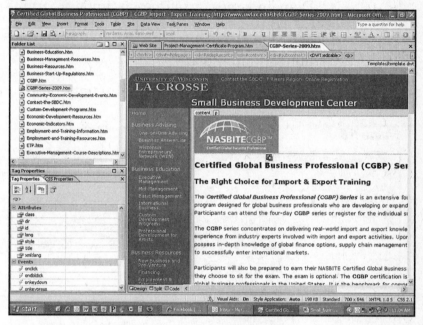

b. Step 2: Then right click on the page's URL from the left side list in order to display the menu options as shown in Figure 5.8. Left click your mouse on the option "Rename."

c. Step 3: The rename option will give you the ability to delete the current URL and type in a new, optimized URL using the keywords you determined to be the most relevant. For example, I will refer back to the earlier fitness example. Any of these URL variations will give Google the opportunity to identify matches in your Page Title, META Keywords, META Description, domain name, full URL, and the content on the actual page:

- Domainname.com/fitnesstrainingprograms
- Domainname.com/Fitnesstrainingprograms-fitnesstrainingplans
- Domainname.com/Fitness-training-programs

Figure 5.8

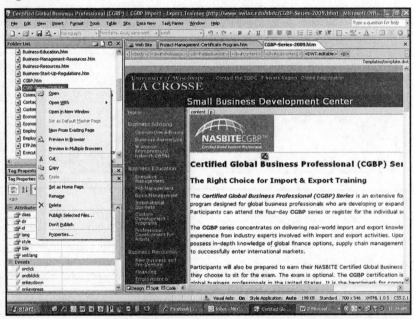

d. Step 4: After you type in the optimized URL, press the "Enter" key on your keyboard. After pressing Enter, you will receive a prompt on your screen similar to what is shown in Figure 5.9. The prompt asks you to confirm you want to update any links to this page that were using the previous URL so the links will not be broken. You should click "Yes."

3. Finally, save the revised HTML file to your Web server to make the URL change live on your Web site.

4. Now repeat the process for all the other content pages you plan to optimize within your Web site.

Figure 5.9

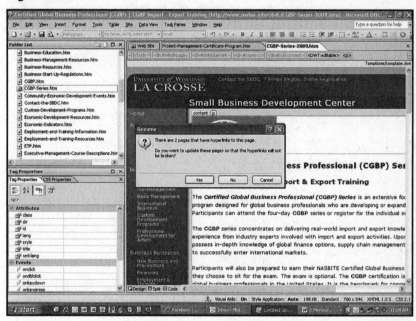

Small Business Owner Optimization Checklist: Part 4

❏ Open your HTML editing software or online development tools used to create your Web site.

❏ Begin by optimizing your page title: highlight all the content that is currently found within <title> and </title> and delete it.

❏ Select the two keywords from your Keyword Tracker Worksheet that are most appropriate for the content page you want to optimize. Type them inside the title code, as in this example: <title>Keyword 1 | Keyword 2</title> separated by a pipe.

❏ Continue by optimizing your META Keywords field: Highlight all the content that is currently found within quotes in the META Keywords field and delete it.

❏ Copy the interior of the custom page title you previously created and paste the content directly into the META Keywords field.

❏ Continue by optimizing your META Description field: Highlight all the content that is currently found within quotes of the META Description field and delete it.

❏ Write a custom META description that is 23 words or less and uses your keywords at least twice.

❏ Continue by optimizing the relevant H-tags: Highlight all the content that is currently found within the H1-tag field and delete it.

Small Business Owner Optimization Checklist: Part 4 *(cont'd)*

❏ Copy the interior of the custom page title you previously created and paste the content directly into the H1-tag field.

❏ Delete the pipe (|) that is currently separating the two keywords and replace it with a hyphen (-) for the H-tag.

❏ <u>Continue by optimizing the URLs of your content pages:</u> Highlight the existing URL for the content page you are optimizing and delete it.

❏ Type in the two keywords you selected for the particular content page into the new URL in one of the three possible variations.

❏ Save the revised HTML file to your Web server in order to make the page title changes live on your Web site.

❏ Update your Sitemap so Google can update its indexing as soon as possible.

❏ Repeat the above checklist for each of the content pages you plan to optimize within your Web site.

❏ Proceed to Chapter 6: Optimize Your Site's Page Content.

CHAPTER 6

Optimize Your Site's Page Content

SEO steps covered in this chapter:

- Step 9: Write specific content pages

- Step 10: Remain within the word count range

- Step 11: Manage keyword prominence, frequency, and density

- Step 12: Use bullet points, bold, italics, and quotation marks

- Step 13: Add anchor text links to content

- Step 14: Optimize ALT tags and file names

Congratulations on finishing Steps 1 through 8 of my 15-step SEO process. In the first eight steps, you were optimizing your content pages essentially behind the scenes. Now it is time to work on the content your visitors actually read within their Web browsers and the content Google indexes. Your visitors will obviously be reading your content to see whether it provides the data or information they were searching for when they found you via Google or another search engine. However, Google is looking for additional matches and consistencies between the content on your page and the custom Page Title, META Keywords, META Description, domain name, URLs, and headings that you just optimized during the previous steps in the process.

I will use this chapter to teach you a specific process for guaranteeing those matches and consistencies are obvious to both your site visitors and to Google, and Google will then reward you with excellent rankings because your content will be highly relevant to the users who just searched on the keywords you are targeting.

The process of optimizing your content will begin by ensuring that the topics within your various content pages are specific, not vague or generalist, and in focus. In addition, your content pages need to adhere to a word-count guideline, and I will give you a range that you can follow. Next, I will show you how to manage your keyword frequency and prominence so you use your keywords often enough and physically place them in the correct positions within your sentences and paragraphs. Finally, I am going to show you how to highlight your keywords by using bullet points, bolding, links, and ALT tags, as well as several other techniques Google values.

Each of the steps in this chapter is short, to the point, and efficient to implement — with the exception of Step 9, which may indicate a need for you to write additional content to supplement what already exists on your content pages. Let us get started.

Step 9: Write specific content pages

Over the last 15 years, I have consulted with hundreds of business owners and executives regarding Web strategy and development. In these consulting sessions, I often uncovered a reoccurring symptom: the client's sites were fulfilling the role of nothing more than generic electronic brochures. But as I said, a generic Web site is only the symptom of a deeper problem. We as business owners are so engaged in our products and services that I think we forget an important point: Our clients or prospective customers may have zero or limited background knowledge about the intricacies of our products and services. So we forget to explain in specific detail the value of our offering. In my opinion, that is why it is so common to find Web sites with content pages about the benefits of the products or services offered using content that is broad and almost generic.

In addition, I have found it common for a small business to list and describe all its products or services on a single content page. The content page may also include a brief, two-sentence description of each product or service with a number to call for more information. Unfortunately, this type of approach can leave visitors, and Google, wondering about the focus of the content page being viewed or indexed.

Instead, Google wants content pages that are specific about one topic only, which is why I recommended the strategy of selecting only two keywords per page during Step 4 of this process. Selecting two keywords per page and creating a specific content page that incorporates those keywords is the perfect strategy because Google will be able to easily identify the matches and consistencies in content. Google will reward you for it as a result.

Generic content pages cannot be effectively optimized, and it is highly unlikely they will rank well in Google because there is too much unrelated information for Google to categorize. The important consistencies that Google relies on are missing.

Therefore, Step 9 in my SEO process recommends that you prepare specific content pages and avoid the temptation to use generic descriptions regarding your products or services, or any other relevant areas about your business. If an aspect of your business is important enough to warrant developing a content page, then make the content specific and focused around the two keywords you selected during Step 4.

Let us go back and look at the **Effectivebehavior.com** Web site as an example to illustrate this recommendation. To create the "Children" screenshot in Figure 6.1, I clicked my mouse on "Our Services" in the horizontal menu underneath the logo in the upper-left corner of the site. A nice list of individual service pages dropped down. I then clicked on "Children" from the Services menu and was taken to a specific content page explaining the details of the service as it relates to children.

Figure 6.1

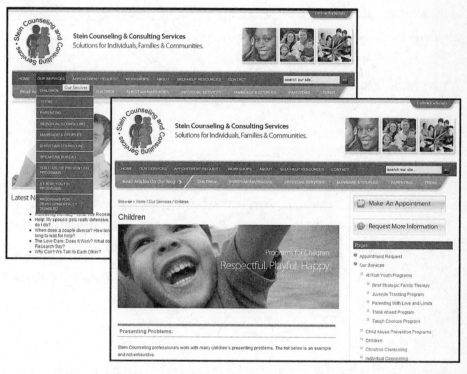

The content on the "Children" page is not generic. It does not attempt to explain all the counseling services for the entire company on one main Services page.

Therefore, if you currently have a "Products" or "Services" page, and you describe all your products or services on these main pages, I recommend you keep the main page, but then add links from the main page to sub-pages for each of the specific products or services your business offers. Then, prepare content for those sub-pages that focuses exclusively on the particular product or service.

Effectivebehavior.com could serve as a guide to follow in case your Web site currently does not include specific content pages. I cannot overemphasize the value of making each of the content pages you plan to optimize as specific as possible and focused around the two keywords you already selected.

Now, here is the optimization process you need to use:

1. Review your Web site with the purpose of identifying any generic content pages.

2. Revise the generic content about a particular product or service so it is more focused. Or, add sub-pages that link from the generic content page and use the sub-pages to provide visitors and Google with the specific content necessary for optimization.

Step 10: Remain within the word count range

As I explained in Step 9, Google prefers specific content pages toward a specific topic, versus vague or general content. In addition, Google prefers that your specific content pages also fit within the parameter of 500 to 1,000 words per page. This is because if your content is too short, you will not have built up enough keyword frequency to highlight your optimization to

Google. If your content is too long, Google will still index it, but if you exceed 1,000 words, the attention span of your site visitors will likely wane. So, the 500 to 1,000 word guideline is exactly that...a guideline to help you balance Google's expectations and the usability needs of your site visitors.

I was recently asked by a participant during my *Best Tactics for Online Marketing* class at the university whether a product-specific page within an e-commerce Web site still needed 500 to 1,000 words. My answer was yes, although the realistic expectation would be to use the lower end of the range. This was a good question, and I added it to the FAQs in Chapter 9 so you can review my complete answer to her and why it is crucial to have content on any page you want to rank well within Google.

I would like to proactively address a potential misperception regarding word count. I realize the 500 to 1,000 words may sound high, but it is not. Let me give you another real-world example to help make this step in the SEO process more tangible.

Figure 6.2 is a screenshot of a content page I developed to promote our Certified Global Business Professional (CGBP) course on campus (you can find the live version of this content page at: **www.uwlax.edu/sbdc/CGBP-Series-2009.htm**). This content page consists of 760 words. The way the content is displayed on the page gives the visual impression it might be longer than it is. But more importantly, it provides Google with the amount of text they consider to be ideal: 500 to 1,000 words. In addition, the content does not discuss the overall international business education programs offered on our campus. The content page focuses specifically on the CGBP designation, which satisfies Step 9 in the SEO process.

Figure 6.2

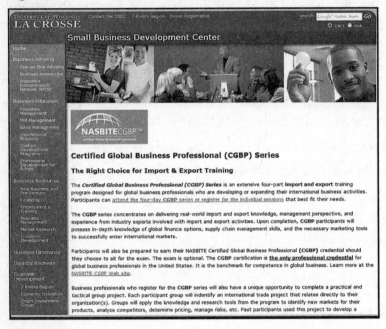

Now, here is the optimization process you need to use:

1. Visit any of the content pages you plan to optimize using your Firefox Web browser.

2. Drag your mouse over the text-based content to highlight it. Then select "Copy" from your browser's "Edit" drop-down menu.

3. Open a Notepad document and "paste" the content you just copied. I am recommending pasting the content into

Notepad before moving it into a Word file because Notepad tends to strip out any odd characters or symbols.

4. Highlight the content in the Notepad file and now copy-paste it into a Microsoft Word document.

5. Then "Select All" by holding down the "CTRL" and "A" keys on your non-Mac keyboard. Select "Apple" and "A" for Mac keyboards Then click on the "Tools" menu and select "Word Count." This will give you the number of words currently on the content page so you can determine how much you need to add in order to reach the 500 to 1,000 word-count range. I suspect if you are currently under 500 words, you could easily increase your word count by simply being more specific regarding the exact value that your product or service provides customers or prospective customers.

6. Open the HTML editing software or online development tools you have used during the earlier steps of the optimization process.

7. Make the content revisions in the actual HTML file and save the revised HTML file to your Web server in order to make the changes live on your Web site.

Step 11: Manage keyword frequency and prominence

In Chapter 1, I defined keyword frequency as the number of times a given keyword or keyword phrase is repeated within the same page of content (not your entire Web site — just the particular page of content being analyzed). Keyword prominence is the determination of how close to the start of a sentence or paragraph a keyword appears. Step 11 will provide some simple guidelines to follow that will ensure your frequency and prominence meet Google's expectations.

Keyword Frequency

I will continue to use the UW-La Crosse CGBP content page as an example. Within the 760 words of content on this page, I repeated the usage of the keyword "CGBP" a total of 32 times. This represents the keyword frequency for this content page.

While a keyword frequency of 32 repetitions seems like a huge number at first, from both a visitor's perspective and Google's, the keyword frequency of 32 is actually quite appropriate. If you visit the live version of the content page (**www.uwlax.edu/sbdc/ CGBP-Series-2009.htm**) you will see for yourself that I did not sacrifice the readability of the content page by achieving such a high frequency.

You will see that I strategically sprinkled the keyword "CGBP" throughout the full 760 words of content — from the top of the page all the way to the bottom. You will find the CGBP keyword in virtually every paragraph throughout the content. The content page still reads nicely, versus clunky as some supposedly "optimized" pages that you have likely read on other Web sites.

Here is a usage guideline to follow when focusing on building your keyword frequency within your content pages. You should strive to reach a keyword frequency of eight to 46. Therefore, your goal should be to use your two keywords a total of eight to 46 times throughout the content page, from top to bottom. Just to be clear, I am not recommending that you use each of the two keywords eight to 46 times for a total keyword usage of 16 to 92. A frequency of 92 would seem ridiculous to users, and Google will begin to become suspicious and potentially consider your content page for keyword stuffing or spamming (both of these terms are defined within the glossary at the back of this book).

So, if your content is closer to 500 words, then your keyword frequency would be closer to eight. If your content is closer to 1,000 words, then your keyword frequency would be closer to 46. Feel free to use the UW-La Crosse Certified Global Business Professional content page as a reference:

- 760 words
- Keyword frequency of 32

Keyword Prominence

On the CGBP content page, whenever possible, I placed the CGBP keyword toward the beginning of sentences, as well as at the beginning of paragraphs. Placing the CGBP keyword "prominently" throughout the content reinforces to Google that the content page is indeed about CGBP, which was also featured within the custom Page Title, META Keywords, META Description, URL, and headings on the content page. This establishes nice consistency. Keyword prominence is a visual observation or measurement. It is not converted into a statistic, like keyword frequency.

As a result of this effort, the UW-La Crosse Certified Global Business Professional page currently ranks No. 8 in Google against more than 60 million competing pages for the keyword "Global Business Professional." The page also ranks No. 10 in Google against 20,100 competing pages. Both of these are fabulous results, especially considering the fact that at the time of this writing, the CGBP content page is only about 60 days old.

Now, here is the optimization process you need to use:

1. Open the HTML editing software or online development tools you have used during the earlier steps of the optimization process.

2. Open the HTML file for the content page you want to optimize using Mozilla Firefox.

3. Click the "CTRL" and "F" keys on your keyboard, and Firefox will display the "Find" search box at the bottom of your browser window, as shown in Figure 6.3.

4. Type your first targeted keyword into the "Find" field and then click the "Highlight All" button, which is the third button from the left.

5. Clicking the "Highlight All" button will visually highlight

each usage of the entered keyword within the content page. You can then easily count each usage, which gives you your current frequency.

6. Revise the content by including additional usages of the targeted keywords in order to achieve a keyword frequency of eight to 46.

7. Focus on placing the new additions of the keywords at the beginning of your sentences and paragraphs in order to increase your keyword prominence.

8. Save the revised HTML file to your Web server in order to make the changes live on your Web site.

Figure 6.3

Step 12: Use bullet points, bold, italics, and quotation marks

Google also pays attention to the way you physically highlight the keywords you are targeting on a particular page. In a similar sense, Google pays attention to your content formatting just like human readers. Because of this, there are four primary ways you can draw Google's attention to your keywords. The following four techniques essentially tell Google during the indexing process, "Slow down... this content is important." The four techniques include:

1. Bullet points
2. Bolding
3. Italics
4. Quotation marks

I will again use the UW-La Crosse Certified Global Business Professional content page as an example to demonstrate these four techniques. You can find the live content page at **www.uwlax. edu/sbdc/CGBP-Series-2009.htm**.

First, you can see that at about one-third of the way down the page, I have included some significant detail about the curriculum of our CGBP course. Instead of leaving all this content in an unruly paragraph of text, I have broken it into bullet points.

Now, bullet points by themselves are not all that unique or special. However, take a look at the last two bullet points in the list. They both include the keyword "CGBP" in order to highlight CGBP's

Figure 6.4

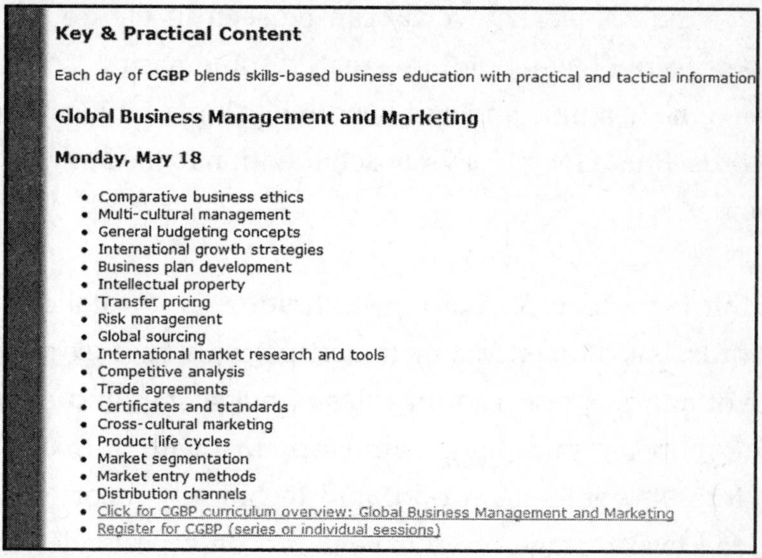

> **Key & Practical Content**
>
> Each day of **CGBP** blends skills-based business education with practical and tactical information
>
> **Global Business Management and Marketing**
>
> **Monday, May 18**
>
> - Comparative business ethics
> - Multi-cultural management
> - General budgeting concepts
> - International growth strategies
> - Business plan development
> - Intellectual property
> - Transfer pricing
> - Risk management
> - Global sourcing
> - International market research and tools
> - Competitive analysis
> - Trade agreements
> - Certificates and standards
> - Cross-cultural marketing
> - Product life cycles
> - Market segmentation
> - Market entry methods
> - Distribution channels
> - Click for CGBP curriculum overview: Global Business Management and Marketing
> - Register for CGBP (series or individual sessions)

importance to Google. Interestingly, I may have inadvertently not followed my own advice here because I could have boosted the keyword prominence for CGBP had I moved these last two bullet points to the top of the list. So instead of being numbers 19 and 20 on the list, the bullet points would be numbers 1 and 2. I have since made that correction on our CGBP content page.

The second content formatting technique I recommend you apply is bolding the keywords you are targeting on your content pages. I confess that the first time I considered using this technique, I thought the content might look odd with a bunch of bolded words sprinkled throughout the page. But it looked just fine. Additionally, the bolding of the keywords visually tells your visitors they are at the right content page and found the perfect page of content that meets their search criteria.

If you visit the CGBP content page, you will see that each of the

32 usages of the keyword have been bolded within the content. Some of the bolded keywords can be seen in Figure 6.5. From my perspective, the bolding creates some visual consistency between the headline and sub-headline (h1 and h2-tags) with the keywords. Plus, Google pays closer attention to the keywords that are bolded.

The third content formatting technique is to italicize your keywords. I recommend using italics sparingly because the formal usage of italics is reserved for titles of magazines and the names of newspapers, ships, and similar items with formal names. Therefore, it would seem odd, and technically incorrect, if you italicized every usage of your keyword on a particular page of content. Let us go back to the CGBP page to review an example. It is likely difficult to see in Figure 6.5, but the only time I used italics on this page was to highlight the title of the program within the first paragraph of content: *Certified Global Business Professional (CGBP) Series*. I simply used bolding for the remaining 31 usages of the CGBP keyword throughout the content page.

Figure 6.5

The fourth and final content formatting technique is to place your keywords in "quotation marks." And similar to the use of italicized words, I recommend that you use quotes only when it is technically appropriate. I suspect the visitors to our CGBP content page would find it odd if all 32 usages of the CGBP keyword looked like this: *"CGBP."* The content would not read smoothly. However, you could include a persuasive testimonial from a customer or client within the content page and place the content within quotation marks. Be sure to incorporate the keywords for the page into the testimonial at least twice. Then place the entire testimonial within quotation marks, which will emphasize the keyword usage to Google. Be sure to keep the testimonial short and to the point. This example would be a perfectly appropriate use of quotation marks to highlight your keywords.

Now, here is the optimization process you need to use:

1. Open the HTML editing software or online development tools that you have used during the earlier steps of the optimization process.

2. Open the HTML file for the content page you want to optimize.

3. Streamline any long paragraphs of text by breaking the text into bullet points. Be sure to include several repetitions of your keywords within the bullet points, similar to the UW-La Crosse CGBP example.

4. Scan your content and bold each repetition of the keywords you are targeting for the particular content page you are optimizing.

5. Be sure you have included keywords into the headers of the content page, as recommended in Step 7 of the process. If you completed Step 7, all you need to do now is italicize the keywords in the headings (H-tags).

6. Add a persuasive client-customer testimonial to your content page. Attempt to include at least two keyword repetitions within the testimonial. Place the testimonial inside quotation marks.

7. Save the revised HTML file to your Web server in order to make the changes live on your Web site.

Step 13: Add anchor text links to content

Anchor text links provide a valuable service to the visitors of your content pages by directing them to additional information that could be valuable to them. Plus, it helps you keep your content pages specific and links visitors to different topics — on equally specific content pages — within your Web site.

From an optimization perspective, Google likes pages with anchor text links because the links give them directions to additional content pages that they may not have had an opportunity to index otherwise. Therefore, Google pays a high degree of attention to the links that you include within your content pages. Consequently, you have an opportunity to get the most value out of your anchor text links by placing keywords within the link text. In fact, I recommend the anchor text links within your content pages never look like the "click here for more details" format that you have likely seen many times, and potentially still use within your Web site. Instead, I will show you how to create anchor text links that provide more value to your visitors, as well as to Google, by following two simple criteria:

1. Include your targeted keywords within the anchor text link at least once.

2. Use up to 15 words within the link in order to make it descriptive for the user and for Google, versus the typical "click here" format.

Look at Figure 6.6 and notice two anchor text links I included as the last two bullet points on the UW-La Crosse CGBP content page. The first link reads: <u>Click for CGBP curriculum overview: Global Business Management and Marketing</u>. This link includes ten words and is descriptive so if a visitor clicks on the link, they have a reasonable expectation of the content they are going to find. Plus, the link also includes one repetition of the CGBP keyword. The second link reads: <u>Register for CGBP (series or individual sessions)</u>. This link is shorter than the first, but it still includes one repetition of the CGBP keyword and provides more SEO value than a link such as "<u>click to register</u>."

Figure 6.6

Key & Practical Content

Each day of **CGBP** blends skills-based business education with practical and tactical information

Global Business Management and Marketing

Monday, May 18

- Comparative business ethics
- Multi-cultural management
- General budgeting concepts
- International growth strategies
- Business plan development
- Intellectual property
- Transfer pricing
- Risk management
- Global sourcing
- International market research and tools
- Competitive analysis
- Trade agreements
- Certificates and standards
- Cross-cultural marketing
- Product life cycles
- Market segmentation
- Market entry methods
- Distribution channels
- Click for CGBP curriculum overview: Global Business Management and Marketing
- Register for CGBP (series or individual sessions)

Now, here is the optimization process you need to use:

1. Open the HTML editing software or online development tools that you have used during the earlier steps of the

optimization process.

2. Open the HTML file for the content page you want to optimize.

3. Revise the current anchor text links on your content page so they meet the two criteria explained above: 1) include your keywords and 2) make each link descriptive.

4. Save the revised HTML file to your Web server in order to make the changes live on your Web site.

Figure 6.7

Step 14: Optimize ALT tags and file names

The final on-page search engine optimization step is to optimize your ALT tags and file names. ALT tags are formally called "attributes." In computing, an attribute is a characterization that defines a property of an object, element, or file. It could be the name or the type of class or extension of a file. Within the context of a content page, ALT tags are used to label and/or briefly describe photos or images within the content. The ALT tags are hidden with the HTML source code of the content page, but they become visible to the visitor when they roll their mouse over a photo or image. The ALT tag then appears for several seconds, displaying the description that was added.

Figure 6.7, a screenshot of the UW-La Crosse CGBP page, is an example of the ALT tag appearing. To create the screenshot, I rolled my mouse over the NASBITE CGBP logo, and the ALT tag appeared. The ALT tag reads: "Certified Global Business Professional (CGBP) Series | CGBP Import – Export Training."

As a side benefit, Google will also index the ALT tags as part of its Google Images services. For example, if you used the Google Images search instead of the standard Web search and searched for Certified Global Business Professional, you would see several of our CGBP-related images ranked No. 1 and No. 2 in the search results. You can access the Google Images feature by clicking "Images" in the upper left corner of the **Google.com** screen. Then, you can enter any keyword you like, and Google will retrieve any images they have indexed relating to your search.

Therefore, I recommend you optimize all the ALT tags on the content pages you have selected for optimization. Your efforts will help increase your rankings within the typical Google search results, and you will see your images rank well within Google's Image search results too.

Figure 6.8

One nice thing about optimizing your ALT tags is that the decision of what content to place within the tag is simple. I will use the ALT tags from our CGBP content page to illustrate. The content includes two graphics — the CGBP logo and the course completion certificate — and a photo of the Holiday Inn in downtown La Crosse, Wisconsin, where attendees will stay during their trip to La Crosse. Following are the actual three ALT tags from the content page:

<img alt="Certified Global Business Professional (CGBP) Series | CGBP Import – Export Training" src="Images%20and%20Forms/Images%20for%20SBDC%20website/logos/nasbite%20logo.jpg" width="210" height="92" />

<img alt="Certified Global Business Professional (CGBP) Series | CGBP Certificate" src="Images%20and%20Forms/Images%20for%20SBDC%20website/logos/certificate.jpg" width="187" height="140" />

<img alt="Certified Global Business Professional (CGBP) Series | CGBP Hotel - Holiday Inn La Crosse" src="Images%20and%20Forms/Images%20for%20SBDC%20website/logos/WELCM_EXTR_02_E.jpg" width="204" height="152" />

The first ALT tag is an exact copy-paste of the Page Title used on the CGBP page, and the second and third ALT tags used the first half of the Page Title, then a vertical pipe (|), repeated the CGBP keywords, and ended with something specific about the photo or image in question. For No. 2, it ended with "CGBP Certificate" and for No. 3, it ended with "CGBP Hotel – Holiday Inn La Crosse."

You will be in good shape if you format your ALT tags in a similar way. But if you open your HTML file to find your ALT tags and do not find any, do not worry. As odd as it may sound, not every Web developer includes ALT tags during the content development process. However, you are welcome to visit the SEO tools section on my Web site to copy-paste the free ALT tag code I made available and paste it into your site code. Then you can optimize each ALT tag from there. Just go to **www.seotrainingproducts. com/seotools**.

ALT tags are also important for people with disabilities because their browser reads the tag and interprets this information back to the user. You can learn the details of how to make your Web site accessible for people with disabilities via the World Wide Web Consortium (W3C) Web site, at **www.w3.org/WAI/EO/Drafts/ PWD-Use-Web/Overview.html**.

In addition to indexing the content within your ALT tags, Google also pays close attention to the file names you have used to save the individual graphics and photos on your content page. For example, if you were to right-click your mouse on the NASBITE CGBP logo on the CGBP content page in an attempt to save it, you would notice the file has been named CGBP.jpeg. I gave the file this name because I know that Google indexes file names as part of it process. File names are the final area where Google looks for consistencies in content.

Now, here is the optimization process you need to use:

1. Open the HTML editing software or online development tools that you have used during the earlier steps of the optimization process.

2. Open the HTML file for the content page you want to optimize.

3. Locate your first ALT tag.

4. Highlight the current text within the ALT tag: <img alt="un-optimized ALT tag content is here but needs to be deleted and replaced with something of value"

5. Now, copy the interior of the custom page title you previously created for this page during Step 4 — i.e., <title>Certified Global Business Professional (CGBP) Series | CGBP Import – Export Training</title> — and paste the content directly into the ALT tag field. Your optimized ALT tag field should now look like this: <img alt="Certified Global Business Professional (CGBP) Series | CGBP Import – Export Training."

6. Locate your second ALT tag and repeat the above process. However, delete the second piece of the Page Title that

follows the vertical pipe (|) and replace it with a keyword and a description of the image — i.e., <img alt="Certified Global Business Professional (CGBP) Series | CGBP Certificate."

7. Continue to repeat this process until all the ALT tags on your content page have been optimized.

8. Next, rename the graphic and photo file names so they include keywords that are relevant to the content page you are optimizing — i.e., CGBP.jpeg, CGBP_Certificate.jpeg, and CGBP_Holiday Inn.jpeg.

9. Save the revised HTML file to your Web server in order to make the changes live on your Web site.

Small Business Owner Optimization Checklist: Part 5

❏ Begin by writing specific content pages: Review your Web site with the purpose of identifying any generic content pages.

❏ Revise generic content about a particular product or service so it is focused and add sub-pages that link from the generic content page.

❏ Remain within the word count: Copy and paste all the text-based content from the page you are optimizing into Notepad and then into a Microsoft Word file.

❏ Run the word count feature in Word to determine whether the page fits within the guideline of 500 to 1,000 words.

❏ Add content to, or delete content from, the page in order to get the word count within the 500 to 1,000-word range.

❏ Manage keyword frequency and prominence: Open the content file you are optimizing via a Mozilla Firefox browser window.

❏ Click the "CTRL" and "F" keys on your keyboard, and Firefox will display the "Find" search box at the bottom of your browser window.

❏ Type your first targeted keyword into the "Find" field, and then click the "Highlight All" button. Count the number of keyword repetitions to determine whether the content currently fits within the recommended range of eight to 46 repetitions, or make necessary adjustments to increase or decrease repetitions.

Small Business Owner Optimization Checklist: Part 5 *(cont'd)*

❑ Place any new keyword additions at the beginning of sentences and paragraphs to increase your keyword prominence.

❑ Use bullet points, bold, italics, and quotation marks: Streamline any long paragraphs of text by breaking the text into bullet points. Be sure to include several repetitions of your keywords within the bullet points.

❑ Scan your content and bold each repetition of the keywords that you are targeting for the particular content page you are optimizing.

❑ Italicize the keywords within the headings (H-tags).

❑ Add a persuasive client-customer testimonial to your content page. Attempt to include at least two keyword repetitions within the testimonial. Place the testimonial inside quotation marks.

❑ Add anchor text links to content: Revise the current anchor text links on your content page so they meet the two criteria explained above: 1) include your keywords and 2) make each link descriptive.

❑ Optimize ALT tags and file names: Copy the interior of the custom page title you previously created during Step 4 and paste it into the ALT tag field. Your optimized ALT tag field should now look like this: <img alt="Certified Global Business Professional (CGBP) Series | CGBP Import – Export Training."

Small Business Owner Optimization Checklist: Part 5 *(cont'd)*

❏ Rename the graphic and photo file names so that they include keywords that are relevant to the content page you are optimizing — i.e., CGBP.jpeg, CGBP_Certificate.jpeg, and CGBP_Holiday Inn.jpeg.

❏ Save the revised HTML file to your Web server in order to make the page title changes live on your Web site.

❏ Proceed to Chapter 7: Accelerate Rankings with Link Building.

CHAPTER 7

Accelerate Rankings with Link Building

SEO steps covered in this chapter:

- Step 15: Leverage articles to power up results

In Chapter 1, I defined both on-page and off-page search engine optimization tactics. You have just completed steps 1 through 14 of my 15-step SEO process, and these first 14 steps of the process dealt exclusively with on-page tactics. In completing the 14 steps, you were directly optimizing the content pages of your Web site.

It is crucial for your content to be in the proper format for Google to index and rank it properly. However, there is another aspect of your Web site that dramatically affects your rankings, and it does not have anything to do with your content pages. Your rankings are impacted to a significant degree by Google's opinion of the popularity of your Web site.

Therefore, now that you have your content in order because of your hard work during steps 1 through 14, it is time to transition to off-page tactics that can help you boost Google's popularity score for your Web site. Investing time toward boosting your site's popularity will enable you to increase your search engine rankings to their highest level possible, and I am about to teach you a process that will increase your site's popularity while adhering to our goal of maximizing efficiency and effectiveness.

Before I cover the specific process, I would like to emphasize several more important points about site popularity. Think of the competition for the top rankings in Google as an accelerated version of the high school popularity contest. Google could look at two identical content pages from competing companies in the same industry, and the Web site that is determined by Google to have the highest level of popularity is the site that will enjoy the highest rankings in the search results.

Google essentially analyzes two main categories of information in determining their search engine rankings:

1. The quality of your content pages and the pages' relevancy to the keywords that were just searched on by a Google user.

Steps 1 through 14 of my SEO process took care of this for you.

2. The number of external or inbound links pointing back to your Web site.

However, Google not only evaluates the number of inbound links pointing back to your Web site, but they also evaluate the popularity of the site that posted the link back to your site. If the site that posted a link back to your Web site is popular, then your site's popularity goes up. If the site has a lower popularity score than your site, there is little to zero increase in your Web site's popularity score. In addition, Google wants to see some similarities between the content on your Web site and the content on the sites that have posted links back to you. For example, it would be of no value to your site's popularity score if I were to post a link on my Web site (**www.seotrainingproducts.com**) back to your Web site, unless you were in the search engine optimization business.

In short, Google has established two main criteria that inbound links must meet in order for the links to have any value toward increasing your Web site's popularity score:

1. Your inbound links must come from Web sites that have an equal or greater popularity score in Google than your Web site.

2. The Web site that posted your link must be in a similar industry, or relevant in some other way to your Web site, so there is a parallel in content between the two sites.

If your inbound links do not meet both of these criteria, Google will score the links as having little value to your Web site. This discourages people from creating links that are of no real value to site visitors, solely for the purpose of increasing site traffic. These irrelevant links are typically created through the use of a "link farm."

So what is a link farm? According to Wikipedia, link farm exchanges were initially conducted informally, but several service companies were created to provide automated registration, categorization, and links to member Web sites. Essentially, a business owner can hire a link farm company to generate hundreds of in-bound links for the business owner's Web site. However, the sites that post the business owner's link are not always credible, and the sites are rarely relevant to the content of the business owner's Web site.

Google does not value the links generated by link farms. Google has even been known to penalize Web sites that employ link farms to generate a high number of irrelevant inbound links. Because of this, I would never recommend that you use a link farm to generate inbound links as part of your strategy to increase your Web site's popularity score.

Offers to boost your number of inbound links for a small fee often come from link farms. It is common for the offers to explicitly state the number of inbound links the service provider will guarantee as a result of the project. I have never read a link farm offer that guaranteed to provide links from Web sites that would actually be relevant to the business owner paying for the service.

Using a link farm is not worth the financial investment. Instead, focus on building high-quality links using the tools you are about to learn in Step 15 of my SEO process. I will show you how to dramatically increase the number of inbound links to your Web site coming from credible sites. Google will reward you for these types of inbound links. And consequently, the popularity of your Web site will soar, as will your search engine rankings. Plus, the process you are about to learn is 110 percent free, as opposed to the $49.95 or potentially higher fees you might pay to a link farm. Save your money, and boost your results in the process.

The first thing you need to do is to take a baseline of the number of inbound links you already have so can measure improvements as a result of your efforts. This baseline will give you the starting point from which you will begin your work. In my opinion, the most efficient way to calculate your baseline number is to use the **SEOBook.com** SEO X-ray tool. Here is the process you will need to use in order to collect the baseline inbound link data:

1. Open a Firefox browser window and go to your Web site's Home Page.

2. Right-click your mouse to activate the on-screen "SEO for Firefox" menu.

3. Click on the "SEO for Firefox" option, located at the bottom of the menu. This will open a sub-menu to the right with the option of "SEO X-ray" at the bottom of the sub-menu.

4. Click on the option "SEO X-ray." This will launch the SEO X-ray tool, which will nearly instantaneously give you an

on-screen dashboard, similar to the one in Figure 7.1.

To create the screenshot shown in Figure 7.1, I went to **www. confidentkidscoach.com** and used the SEO X-ray tool as described. For Step 15 in the SEO process, we are only interested in the number of "external" or inbound links listed at the top of the screenshot. In this example, there are 865 inbound links pointing back to **www. confidentkidscoach.com**. Not a bad baseline to begin with.

Please go ahead and repeat this process on your Home Page, and then you will have your baseline of inbound links

Figure 7.1

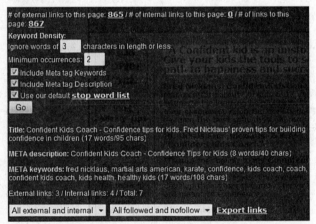

Step 15: Add articles to power up your results

Now that you have your baseline number of inbound links, let us explore how you should efficiently, effectively increase the number of inbound links that direct visitors back to your Web site and how you can ensure the Web sites posting links back to your site will have similarities in content to yours. While this may sound like a significant challenge, it is actually going to be quite easy to satisfy both of these expectations. We will use a process called "link building."

I recommend you first create an "Articles" or "Resources" content section on your Web site. This new content section will be the home to articles that you personally write, as well as other articles that you think would be relevant to your site's visitors. Yes, I am recommending that you begin writing articles. The articles I am suggesting would be approximately 500 to 1,000 words in length. I recommend that you write a few short articles of 500 to 1,000 words that demonstrate your expertise with respect to the products and services you provide, or the industry you represent. Your taking time to write articles will boost your credibility and expertise among your Web site visitors. You will likely be amazed at the reaction people give you when they know you are an author. And most importantly, the majority of your Web site visitors will be impressed to see that you have written articles on the topics they are interested in learning more about. I believe it is impossible to overestimate the value that several high-quality articles can add to your Web site.

To help put this recommendation into perspective, I encourage you to visit: **www.7riversmarketplace.com/SS/Page.aspx?sstarg=&facing=false&secid=62570&artid=1065326** to read a recent article I wrote for one of the business magazines in southwest Wisconsin. The name of the magazine is *The River Valley Business Report*, and the article is less than 700 words. It is focused and to the point — a good example of the type of article I recommend that you write.

If you are comfortable in your writing skills, then my

recommendation of writing a few articles probably fits well into your skill set. However, if you do not consider yourself a good writer, please do not let my recommendation cause you any anxiety. I understand that writing is not for everyone, and that for some people, the proverbial blank sheet of paper or computer screen can be aggravating. If you prefer not to write, then I recommend you consider either outsourcing the writing assignment to a freelance writer in your local area or hiring a freelancer via **www. elance.com** to complete the articles for you. This is called "ghost writing," and the link-building results will be exactly the same whether you wrote the articles yourself or hired a freelance ghost writer to do it for you.

You will likely need to pay a freelance writer anywhere between $300 and $500 for each 500 to 1,000 word article written for you. Make sure you also receive a copyright release from the freelancer so you have permission to post it onto your Web site, or any other site you choose. This will ensure you are free to distribute the article throughout the Internet to boost the inbound links to your Web site.

I am recommending that you write articles because these assets are tremendously valuable to link building. A few well-written articles will be all that you need in order to recruit hundreds — or even thousands — of inbound links to your Web site. There is no limit to the number of inbound links you could generate with five to ten high-quality articles.

Once you have written the articles, or received them back from your freelancer, I recommend you post the articles immediately to your Articles or Resources section within your Web site. This will ensure that Google has an opportunity to index your new article content. Plus, be sure to update your Sitemap so that Google can find the new content as efficiently as possible.

Next, I recommend you open accounts as an author at two different, and totally free, Web sites that will help you distribute your articles throughout the Internet. The two Web sites can be found at:

- **www.IdeaMarketers.com**
- **www.Ezinearticles.com**

I have used both of these sites many times, and they are excellent, user-friendly, and deliver outstanding link-building results. Both sites have helped me generate thousands of links via the articles I have written. **IdeaMarketers.com** was created by Marnie Pehrson, who has done an amazing job in creating a real asset for small business owners who are looking for high-quality content to post on their Web sites, or a vehicle to distribute the articles they have written.

IdeaMarketers.com says the following about their Web site: "IdeaMarketers.com is a writer-publisher matching service where writers can post their articles for free to gain exposure to 1,000s of online and offline publishers. People can request to reprint your article and when you agree to let them, your name, bio, and a link to your site will be included. This helps increase link popularity to your site. Not only that, but our site receives approximately two million page views per month and is regularly spidered by

Google, MSN and others. This means prominently placed articles on our site are spidered and links on them are followed. Writing articles is a great way to establish yourself as an expert in your field by writing about your area of expertise and getting free publicity back to your Web site."

The reprinting of your articles that was mentioned in the preceding quote is sometimes referred to as "syndication." Syndication will be your greatest tool during the link-building process. Via **IdeaMarketers.com** and **Ezinearticles.com**, you will give Web site owners around the world access to your articles so they can post your content freely on their Web site. And whenever a site owner posts your article to their Web site, and it is indexed by Google, this counts as another inbound link for you because your articles will all include a link to your Web site at the bottom of the text. With each article posting, your Web site's popularity score increases.

Furthermore, it can be the same article posted thousands of times on different Web sites. This is why I recommended you get started with just two articles. In a short period of time — 90 days or less — you will be able to go back and check the number of inbound links via the SEO X-ray tool and evaluate the results. I am confident that the increase in inbound links will motivate you to either write more articles or get in touch with your freelance writer again.

Building inbound links in this manner increases your popularity score because it is highly likely that only site owners who have Web sites similar in content to yours will be interested in posting your articles. Otherwise, your content would not have any relevancy to their site visitors. Therefore, you have fulfilled one of Google's primary criteria to inbound links: the links must come from sites that are relevant to your Web site.

The **IdeaMarketer.com** Web site also provides site owners with the ability to download articles from authors across 20 different topic categories. Plus, these 20 topics also include 204 sub-categories. That means you have many opportunities to write articles in a wide variety of categories. Following is a comprehensive list of all the categories and sub-topics for which **IdeaMarketers.com** accepts articles, so you can get a sense for the opportunities ahead.

Architecture/Construction

Autos

Business

- Accounting
- Authoring
- Career Change
- Coaching Business
- Communication
- Corporate
- Customer Service
- E-Business
- Entrepreneur
- Joint Ventures

- Getting Started Online
- Healthcare
- Home Business
- How to Charge
- Human Resources
- Legal
- Management
- Multiple Income Streams
- Non-Profit
- Organization
- Outsourcing & Delegation

- Professional Forums
- Public Speaking
- Real Estate
- Self Employment
- Small-Med
- Trucking/Truck Driving
- Worker's Comp

Entertainment

- Entertainment
- Art/Antiques
- Books
- Children's Books
- Children's Movies
- Fishing
- Games
- Humor
- Movies/Film
- Music
- Parties
- Recreation
- Sci-Fi
- Storytelling
- Sports
- Television

Computers/Tech

- Blogging
- Affiliate Revenue
- Audio Streaming
- Autoresponders
- Cellular
- Domain Names
- Digital Cameras
- Ecommerce
- Email Marketing
- Ezine Publishing
- Fax
- Hardware Reviews
- Hardware Tips
- Internet
- Identity Theft
- News
- Podcasting
- PPC Advertising
- SEO
- Social Bookmarking
- Social Media
- Software Reviews
- Software Tips

- Training
- Trends
- Video
- VOIP
- Web Design
- Writing for Web

Education

- Adult/Continuing
- Childhood
- College
- Distance Learning
- Home Schooling

Finances/Money

- Employment
- Financial Freedom
- Financial Wellness
- Foreclosures
- Home
- How to Cut Expenses
- Investing
- Mortgages/HELOC
- Personal
- Planning
- Real Estate Investing

- Taxes
- Tax Lien Investing
- Wealth Building

Gifts/Special Occasions

Glamour & Beauty

Home/Family/Parenting

- Arts/Crafts
- Emergency Preparedness
- Interior Design/ Decorating
- Family/Family History
- Flowers
- Food
- Gardening
- Holidays
- Marriage
- Moving
- Parenting Children
- Parenting Teens
- Pets
- Recipes

Home Improvement

- Air & Water Purification
- Appliances
- Baths
- Carpentry
- Carpets & Floors
- Cleaning
- Contractors, Construction
- Drywall & Insulation
- Electrical
- Energy Efficiency
- Furnishings
- Garages
- Heat & Air
- Home Safety, Health
- Home Security
- Interior Design/ Decorating
- Kitchens
- Landscaping/Yards
- Lighting & Fixtures
- Miscellaneous
- Patios, Decks, Sunrooms
- Pest Control
- Plumbing

- Pools & Spas
- Roofing & Gutters
- Septic and Sewers
- Siding Awnings & Shutters
- Water Damage Repair

Humanities/Writing

- Humanities
- Academics
- Cultures
- Education
- Writing

Self-Help/Lifestyle

- Abusive Relationships
- Alcoholism
- Alternative Healthcare
- Career
- Dating
- Dentist/Orthodontist
- Diabetes
- Elder Care
- Emotional Wellness
- Energy Healing
- Food/Wine

- Health Nutrition Fitness
- Intuition
- Leadership
- Life Balance
- Life Purpose
- Inspirational
- Law of Attraction
- Lifestyles
- Meditation
- Men's Issues
- Motivational
- Nature
- Natural Health
- Organization
- Prosperity
- Psychology
- Psychology of Eating
- Simplify Your Life
- Spirituality
- Relationships
- Religious Prophecy
- Religious, Christian
- Religious, Non-Christian
- Romance

- Self-Defense
- Self-Help
- Shopping
- Time Management
- Vegan/Vegetarian
- Women's Issues

Marketing

- Article Marketing
- Attraction Marketing (Law of Attraction)
- Affiliate Marketing
- Advertising
- Branding
- Copywriting

Ebooks

- Networking
- Information Marketing
- List Building/Product Launches
- Marketing 101
- Marketing Plans & Implementation
- Niche Marketing
- Off-line/Telemarketing

- Online

- PR/Media

- Sales

- Shoestring

- Visibility

News

- Good News

- News

- Current Events

Parties, Decorations

Political

- Conservative

- Liberal

- Satire

Self-Publishing

Travel/Tourism

The sign-up processes for both **IdeaMarketers.com** and **Ezinearticles.com** are easy and can be completed quickly. I will cover the highlights of the IdeaMarketers.com sign-up process to make sure some important points are properly covered. Here is the process you will need to follow to complete your free sign up.

Figure 7.2

1. Go to **IdeaMarketers.com** and familiarize yourself with the Web site's main navigation, which is located near the top center of the page.

2. Drag your mouse over the "Writers" tab and a yellow drop-down menu will appear, as shown in Figure 7.2.

3. Click on "Signup" and you will be taken to the page where you can complete the brief sign-up form, shown in Figure 7.3.

Figure 7.3

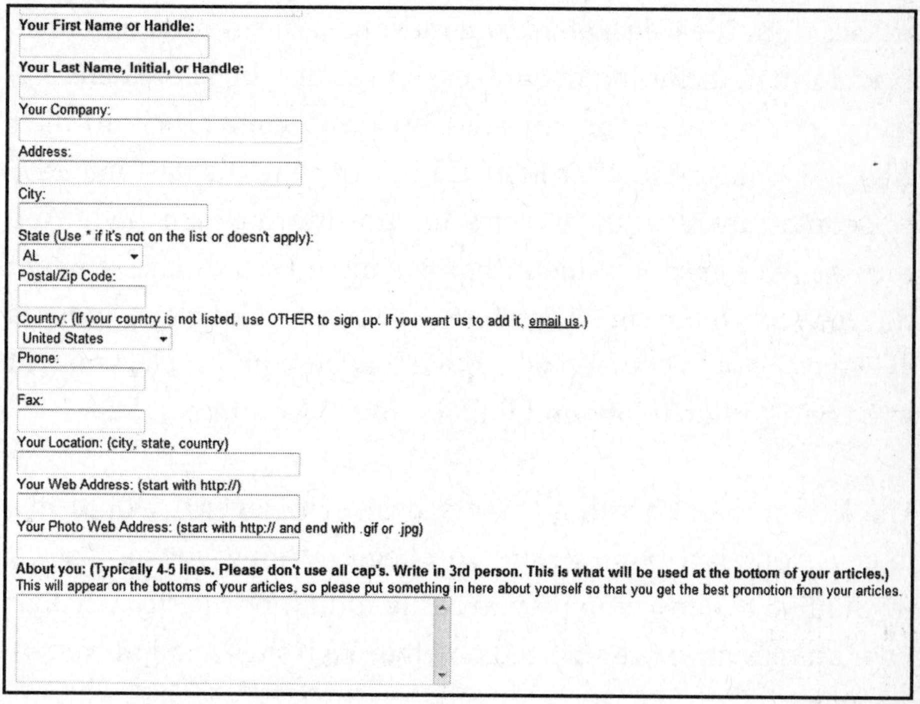

Your First Name or Handle:

Your Last Name, Initial, or Handle:

Your Company:

Address:

City:

State (Use * if it's not on the list or doesn't apply):
AL ▼
Postal/Zip Code:

Country: (If your country is not listed, use OTHER to sign up. If you want us to add it, email us.)
United States ▼
Phone:

Fax:

Your Location: (city, state, country)

Your Web Address: (start with http://)

Your Photo Web Address: (start with http:// and end with .gif or .jpg)

About you: (Typically 4-5 lines. Please don't use all cap's. Write in 3rd person. This is what will be used at the bottom of your articles.)
This will appear on the bottoms of your articles, so please put something in here about yourself so that you get the best promotion from your articles.

For the "About you" field, at the bottom of the form, pay attention to the instructions, as the "About You" information is critical to your link-building efforts.

Here is an example for the "About You" information that you can modify however you like: [Insert your company name here] followed by your description of four to five sentences that explains what your company is all about, your services, your products, and perhaps even where you are located. [Insert your company name here] can be found online at [insert your full Web site domain name here].

In addition, **IdeaMarketers.com** places your link next to your four- or five-sentence profile. Web site owners that download articles from **IdeaMarketers.com** must post the information in its exact format, including the link back to your Web site. Therefore, every time someone downloads and posts your article to their Web site, you get another inbound link. Again, the vast majority of people downloading articles for posting on their own Web sites are looking for content that is similar to the other content currently on their site. Therefore, as soon as Google re-indexes the Web site of the person who downloaded your article, you will score an additional inbound link for your Web site.

The key is to get writing those articles. However, I would like to cover one last point before you begin writing your articles. I would like to show you how to easily monitor or verify whether your articles have been posted on other Web sites and indexed by Google.

All you need to do is a Google search on each of your specific article titles to find all the sites where the articles have been indexed.

In addition, you can also Google yourself using an exact-match search to see how many indexed pages are dedicated to you as an author. The number of Google pages that come up when I Google "Stephen Woessner" fluctuates anywhere between 400 to 800 pages as content is refreshed and Google does re-indexing. This eliminates old links and sites that have since been abandoned or are otherwise invalid. Figure 7.4 shows an example of the most recent Google result for me. The No. 2-ranked Web site is an example of a site owner downloading an article from **Ezinearticles.com** and posting it to their Web site. I wrote this article several years ago while working in the private sector, and Google still considers it to be relevant content. So not only will link-building activities boost your Web site's popularity score, you will be adding long-lasting links back to your site.

Figure 7.4

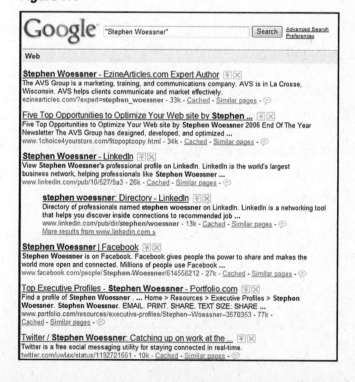

Small Business Owner Optimization Checklist: Part 6

☐ Use the SEO X-ray tool to take a baseline of the number of your current total of inbound links.

☐ Add an Articles or Resources section to the main navigation of your Web site. Write two or three articles related to your products, services, or the industry you represent.

☐ Or, if writing articles is not your preference, hire a local freelancer or someone via **www.elance.com** to complete the writing for you. Get a copyright release.

☐ Upload the articles to the Articles or Resources section on your Web site.

☐ Update your Sitemap.

☐ Sign up for free author accounts at **IdeaMarketers.com** and **Ezinearticles.com**.

☐ Upload your articles to both **IdeaMarketers.com** and **Ezinearticles.com**.

☐ Each month, conduct exact-match Google searches on your article titles, as well as your first and last name, to see the list of Web sites that have posted your content.

☐ Use the SEO X-ray tool to measure your number of inbound links each month.

☐ Proceed to Chapter 8: More Small Business Owner FAQs.

More Small Business Owner FAQs

I mentioned earlier that I teach a popular search engine optimization class at the University of Wisconsin-La Crosse. Each time I teach the class, the small business owners in attendance always ask some excellent questions. I have tried to capture as much of the Q&A content as possible here so that it can serve as an additional resource to you.

Q: Does Google index content within Microsoft Word®, Microsoft PowerPoint®, and PDF files?

A: Yes, absolutely. Google does a good job indexing Word, PowerPoint, and PDF files. If you have some good content within these file formats, I strongly recommend you add it to your Web site right away so Google can index the content. For example, I conducted an exact-match search for "marketing case studies" in Google, which generated the results shown in Figure 8.1. Now look at the content page that is ranked No. 7 in the results. The clickable link in the results reads: (PDF) Top 5 Search Marketing Case Studies. Notice that (PDF) is the first thing listed at the beginning of the link. Google places the (PDF) at the front-end of the link so users know if they click on the link, they will open a PDF file instead of an HTML content page. In addition, the content page's URL that is placed underneath the META Description ends in .pdf.

Figure 8.1

Q: *Will Google index keywords that are placed at the bottom of my site pages and colored in white over my white background so site visitors can't see them? I heard this works with search engines.*

A: No, this technique is a form of what is called "keyword stuffing." Google does not like this type of tactic. Keyword stuffing is also sometimes referred to as "keyword spamming." Keyword stuffing or spamming is considered a black-hat SEO tactic. You can read more about Black Hat SEO within the glossary at the back of this book. But the short story is Google has been known to blacklist or delist Web sites from its rankings when the sites were found to be using Black Hat SEO tactics. To rank well within its search results, Google simply wants you to focus on developing high-quality content and using legitimate SEO tactics. Every single step in the 15-step SEO process you just learned in this book is 100 percent legitimate.

Q: *Should I try to optimize the content of my Home Page, or should I just use the Home Page to steer visitors to the right content pages within my site?*

A: I understand that some business owners prefer to keep their Home Page content more general in nature, versus specifically targeting two keywords, as I recommended during the 15-step SEO process. However, I am a firm believer that to not optimize your Home Page is a missed opportunity. I propose a compromise. I suggest you still use your Home Page to target two keywords that reflect your business at a comprehensive level versus a specific product or service. The keywords should still fit the selection parameters covered in Chapter 4. Plus, the content you place on your Home Page should follow the steps you learned during Chapters 5 and 6.

As a final step, I recommend that you strategically place about five to ten links to other content areas within your Web site throughout your Home Page. These five to ten links will create balance between your optimization goals and the need to encourage your site's visitors to learn about the specific products and services your business can provide.

Q: *Do increases in site traffic help boost search engine rankings?*

A: Not directly. However, you can keep your customers and prospects coming back to your Web site by consistently creating new content. Additionally, keeping your content fresh and updated will increase Google's opinion of your Web site. You can learn more about this topic by looking up the word "Age" in the glossary at the back of this book. Within the glossary, Aaron Wall, owner of SEOBook.com, provides an interesting discussion of how the age of your content can affect your search engine rankings.

Q: *What is the different between Black Hat and White Hat SEO?*

A: Black Hat SEO tactics are tactics that essentially attempt to outthink Google and other search engines by using deceptive tactics to pull the wool over the eyes of algorithms in an attempt to artificially boost a site's search engine rankings. As a result, sites that employ Black Hat tactics run the risk of being delisted by Google and other search engines. However, White Hat SEO is the use of 100 percent legitimate tactics that search engines appreciate. Here again, Aaron Wall, owner of **SEOBook.com**, provides good definitions of both within the glossary of this book. Rest assured that all 15-steps in my SEO process are legitimate, White Hat techniques.

Q: My Web developer wants to redesign my Web site using Cascading Style Sheets and says that it will make my site more search-engine friendly. Is that true?

A: I have not read anything about Cascading Style Sheets (CSS) providing the additional benefit of increased search-engine friendliness. That does not mean you should not consider using CSS if you are planning a site redesign. I say that because cascading style sheets will increase the efficiency and effectiveness of your content management process. For example, the efficiencies are essentially gained in navigation changes so that if you make a change in one place (add a new section into your menus), the change is automatically replicated throughout the Web site. Or, if you change a logo in the site header, it appears now on every single page, versus having to make many manual updates. But cascading style sheets by themselves do not make your Web site more Google-friendly. You can read more about cascading style sheets in the **SEOBook.com** glossary at the back of this book.

Q: *Does buying multiple domain names and redirecting traffic to a main domain provide any search engine optimization benefits?*

A: No. In order for a domain name to have value from a search engine optimization perspective, the domain needs to represent a content-rich Web site, not a simple redirect of traffic. Therefore, redirecting traffic over to a different Web site does not provide any SEO benefits.

However, buying multiple domain names and funneling traffic into a main Web site is still a good online promotional strategy, even though it does not provide SEO benefits. Years ago, I learned that General Mills owned 3,000 different domain names in order to protect the names of their brands and to redirect traffic. I suspect they own many more domain names now. If you find a domain name you are interested in, go ahead and buy it, and redirect the traffic to your main Web site.

Q: *What if my Web site only has about five content pages? Should I even bother optimizing a small site like mine?*

A: Absolutely. I recommend that you optimize the five content pages that you do have and invest some time and effort toward developing additional content pages. Please refer back to Chapter 6 to review the process of developing content pages that are topic-specific and highly focused around the keywords you selected as part of Chapter 4. In addition, a highly efficient, effective way to boost the amount of content on your Web site is to post articles you think would be relevant to your visitors. If you do not have the time you will need to write your own articles, then I recommend you visit **ezinearticles.com** and **ideamarketers.com** (discussed in Chapter 7) to search for articles that would be relevant. Then post each article you find onto your Web site.

Remember, you must keep the site credit and author information intact so you are providing a link back to the article's author. The tactic of adding these articles is an excellent way to expand your Web site's content without investing the time toward original content development. Plus, you can then optimize the articles once they are posted on your Web site using the 15-step process you just learned. This will bring even more visitors to your Web site.

Q: What if my Web site is new within the last six months? What should be my most important priority for increasing my search engine rankings and number of unique visitors?

A: I recently encountered an identical situation in working one-on-one with a client at the UW-La Crosse Small Business Development Center. The business owner had launched a new Web site within the last six months. The site was created by one of our local Web site development firms, and from what I could tell, the company did a nice job.

However, even after six months, this business owner's Web site only had one inbound link pointing back to her Web site. Plus, the popularity score of her Web site, according to Google PageRank, was a big zero out of 10. While every Web site begins with a popularity score of zero, the key is to launch the site with the objective of building popularity as quickly as possible.

The good news is that fixing the zero popularity score is relatively easy. This business owner happened to be a prolific writer, but she had not taken the time to write articles suitable for posting onto her Web site. The articles she tends to write are for other uses, like magazines. During our meeting, I recommended that she take the time to write two or three articles ASAP, and then post the articles onto her Web site. I then recommended that she distribute her articles throughout the Internet as part of the link-building process explained in Chapter 7. I affirmed that if she were to write the articles and distribute them as I had recommended, she would likely earn about 90 to 100 inbound links within 90 days or less.

Q: Does Google have the capability to index dynamically generated content pages?

A: First, I will define "dynamically generated content" for those readers who may not be familiar with the term. Dynamically generated content means that these pages (i.e., product pages on an e-commerce Web site or articles on a media Web site) are stored in a database and do not actually exist on the Web server until a site visitor requests the information. The product page is then dynamically created and served up to that person. A dynamically generated content page is easy to spot within the URL of the browser window because you will always see some sort of reference that looks like ID=809. The 809 could be any number, but there will always be the ID=(some number). The number — 809 in this example — is the location of the product, article, or other item within the database and where the Web server needs to go in order to retrieve the data and create the page for the visitor.

Second, and to directly answer the question, yes, Google does index dynamically generated content. However, during the most recent offering of the *Best Tactics for Online Marketing* class I teach at the University of Wisconsin-La Crosse, one of the participants asked me to review one of her dynamically generated product pages. We did, and I noticed that Google had not indexed the page when I tested the page using the Google PageRank cached snapshot of page feature. Then we moved to another product page and discovered that Google had indexed the second product page just fine. Because I am not a database administrator or developer, I recommended that she contact the Web development company she had worked with to develop the Web site and explain what she had discovered. The Web developers could likely make adjustments to the database structure. Clearly something was not right with one of the products.

Finally, do not be reluctant to add dynamic content to your Web site. It is highly likely that Google will index your dynamic content just fine. However, I recommend that you ask the database developer you plan to work with to demonstrate their experience in designing Google-friendly database structures so you have the assurance you are working with someone who is familiar with best practices.

Q: If Google does not index image-based links, is it okay to have a clickable button or graphic on a page that links to a contest or some other promotional type page?

A: Absolutely, because this type of design element is visually attractive and your visitors may be more likely to click on the graphic or image than a text-based link. So from a design perspective, I say go for it. However, I recommend that you also add a link to the contest or promotional content page to your Sitemap as well as add the page to your indexable navigation. These steps will ensure that the clickable button is not the only way your site visitors, and Google for that matter, will be able to find the content page. If you do not add the links to your Sitemap and navigation, you may be cheating yourself out of another indexed page in Google, and consequently, some traffic from visitors who may be interested in your content.

Q: I am concerned about your recommendation of building a keyword frequency of eight to 46 times on one content page. This seems a bit excessive. Will using my two keywords that much on one content page make my text read clunky or seem "over optimized" to my site visitors?

A: I completely understand this concern. I would never recommend that anyone create a content page that reads silly or looks in any way unprofessional to their site visitors. The impression your site visitors have of your content is critical.

However, if your content page is between 500 and 1,000 words, your content will read just fine if you increase your keyword frequency to the eight to 46 repetitions that I recommend. If your content is closer to 500 words, then you should be closer to eight repetitions, and then the reverse is true for pages that are closer to 1,000 words. You should be able to get closer to 46 repetitions by having 1,000 words to work with. I encourage you to try one page and then judge for yourself whether readability has been compromised once you see it in black and white.

I encourage you to trust the 15-step SEO process you have spent time studying, and then test the results. I suspect that you will be pleasantly surprised.

Q: I went to use the free XML-Sitemaps.com tool you recommended. However, I noticed before using it that the free version of the tool only works for Web sites that have less than 500 pages. If our Web site includes links to other sites (i.e., distributors, vendors, or industry associations), does the XML-Sitemaps.com tool follow those links and then count those pages against our

500-page limit?

A: No, the only pages that count toward your 500-page limit are the pages that are hosted for your domain on your Web site. The XML-Sitemaps.com tool will not follow links that are external to your domain/Web site. Links you post on your Web site, such as those to distributors, vendors, or associations, will not be a factor.

Q: *How can I use search engine optimization to weed out the tire kickers from coming into my Web site?*

A: This is a wonderful question that directly connects conversions to search engine optimization. Conversion essentially means getting your site visitors to take some form of action — i.e., place an order or sign up for a newsletter. Most e-commerce sites will experience a conversion rate of between 2 and 4 percent of unique visitors. Meaning, of all unique visitors traveling through a Web site, approximately 2 to 4 percent of them will convert by taking some form of action. There is a definition of conversion in the glossary of this book.

With that said, you can absolutely use several of the SEO steps in this process to reduce the number of untargeted visitors entering your Web site. The more highly focused your Page Titles and META Descriptions fields are, the less likely you will be to get bad traffic. When a user searches in Google for a content page, and they see your Web site within the search results, you have an opportunity to display a highly-targeted Page Title that links back to the content page on your site, which the person may be seeking. Plus, you can reinforce their potential interest by writing a specific, keyword-focused META Description (23 words or less that uses your keywords twice). If your Page Title and/or META Description appeals to the Google searchers, they will click on your link. If not, then they will move on to someone else's site.

Q: *I understand we should use the Keyword Targeting Ratio to help identify the best proven performers. However, what if a keyword that has the lowest ratio also has a low number of daily searches, let us say 50 daily searches according to the SEOBook.com Keyword Suggestion Tool, versus a keyword that has higher ratio, but its daily searches are 300 or more? Plus, both keywords being evaluated have ratios less than 500, as you recommended. Would it be okay to target the keyword that has a higher ratio, but also has the higher number of daily searches?*

A: Absolutely, and this is the type of judgment call and business decision you should consider making when optimizing your site's content pages. The key to excellent keyword selection is to choose the keywords with the lowest ratios because you will be more efficient and effective in scoring high rankings in Google for these words. With that said, there will be occasions when it will make strategic sense to push the upper end of the ratio in order to give your Web site the opportunity to substantially increase unique visitors via a high-volume keyword or two.

Q: *Do I still need 500 to 1,000 words of text-based content on product-specific pages within an e-commerce Web site?*

A: The first step is to test and verify the indexing of your product pages to make sure that Google is not experiencing any difficulties with indexing the current content. It is common for e-commerce sites to use dynamically generated product pages because the product information is managed via a database. And sometimes, dynamic-based content can inadvertently cause indexing problems for Google.

Assuming that the product pages are being indexed properly, then yes, I do recommend that you try to reach the 500 word count on those pages. I recently worked with a participant during my *Best Tactics for Online Marketing* class on campus regarding this specific issue. We visited the No. 1 selling product page on her Web site, and I was stunned to find it contained little information. However, because there was not much information on this top-selling product's page, the company could likely make significant increases in its online conversion rate by adding some high-quality, descriptive content. Therefore, I recommended that she add some content that emphasized the product's points of differentiation, product specifications, usages, why a customer should order the product from her company versus a competitor, and other details.

She was stunned. She went from not knowing what the company could use for additional content and transitioned to understanding, from a marketing perspective, all the missed opportunities. And all the new content that she would add could be latent with the two keywords about the product in question.

Q: *Why is so much of the information that is out there about SEO so contradictory?*

A: I completely agree, and it was frustrating to me as I was beginning my educational journey in studying SEO. I quickly decided I needed to find out for myself what worked and what did not, once I had a general sense of SEO practices from the books and other forms of literature I studied. Besides, I am a practitioner, and I like to experiment to see what works and what does not. Therefore, my goal was to provide you with as unbiased of a resource as possible that is based on my experience in the private sector as well as on campus. While you may find contradictions to some of the material you have studied from other sources, I simply ask you to trust that this process works. And trust in the fact that I have ensured your results with a 110 percent money back guarantee when you use this book and its companion DVD together.

Instead of worrying about contradictions, focus on increasing your efficiency and effectiveness. This 15-step process will help you accomplish both.

YOUR COMPANY®
Your **Slogan**

HOME / ABOUT US / PRODUCT /

Your **Slogan** Find more >

> About **Company**

User name [ ]
Password [ ] Log in

Name:
[ ]

Address:
[ ]

Your text:
[ ]

World

Up time zdfbbhkj drtgfgbf gv
dtyterfg ghjgj rtyghj.

Zdfbbhkj drtgfgbf gvb fgdfh
dfgg fghty te dfb j rtyghj.

Glossary of SEO-related Terms, courtesy of SEOBook.com

The following glossary of SEO-related terms was reprinted with permission of Aaron Wall, owner of **SEOBook.com**.

A

Above the Fold

A term traditionally used to describe the top portion of a newspaper. In e-mail or Web marketing, it means the area of content viewable prior to scrolling. Some people also define "above the fold" as an ad location at the top of the screen, but due to banner blindness, typical ad locations do not perform as well as ads that are well integrated into content. If ads look like content, they typically perform much better.

See also: Google AdSense heat map — shows ad click-through

rate estimates based on ad positioning.

AdWords

Google's advertisement and link auction network. Most of Google's ads are keyword targeted and sold on a cost-per-click basis in an auction, which factors in ad click-through rate as well as max bid. Google is looking into expanding their ad network to include video ads, demographic targeting, affiliate ads, radio ads, and traditional print ads.

AdWords is an increasingly complex marketplace. One could write a 300-page book just covering AdWords.

Affiliate Marketing

Affiliate marketing programs allow merchants to expand their market reach and mindshare by paying independent agents on a cost-per-action (CPA) basis. Affiliates only get paid if visitors complete an action.

Most affiliates make next to nothing because they are not aggressive marketers, have no real focus, fall for wasting money on instant wealth programs that lead them to buying a bunch of unneeded garbage via other's affiliate links, and do not attempt to create any real value.

Some power affiliates make hundreds of thousands or millions of dollars per year because they are heavily focused on automation and/or tap large traffic streams. Typically, niche affiliate sites make more per unit effort than overtly broad ones because they are easier to focus (and thus have a higher conversion rate).

Selling a conversion is typically harder than selling a click (like AdSense does, for instance). Search engines are increasingly looking to remove the low-quality affiliate sites from the search results through the use of algorithms, which detect thin affiliate sites and duplicate content; manual review; and, implementation of landing page quality scores on their paid ads.

See also:

- Commission Junction: probably the largest affiliate network
- Linkshare: another large affiliate network
- Performics: another large affiliate network
- Azoogle Ads: ad offer network focused on high margin / high profit verticals
- CPA Empire: similar to AzoogleAds
- Amazon Associates: Amazon's affiliate program
- Clickbank: an affiliate network for selling electronic products and information

Age

Some social networks or search systems may take site age, page age, user account age, and related historical data into account when determining how much to trust that person, Web site, or document. Some specialty search engines, like blog search engines, may also boost the relevance of new documents.

Fresh content that is also cited on many other channels (like related blogs) will temporarily rank better than you might expect because many of the other channels that cite the content will cite it off their home page or a well-trusted, high PageRank page. After those sites publish more content and the reference page falls into their archives, those links are typically from pages that do not have as much link authority as their home pages.

Some search engines may also try to classify sites to understand what type of sites they are, as in news sites or reference sites that do not need updates that often. They may also look at individual pages and try to classify them based on how frequently they change.

See also: Google Patent 20050071741: Information retrieval based on historical data — mentions that document age, link age, link bursts, and link churn may be used to help score the relevancy of a document.

Analytics

Software which allows you to track your page views, user paths, and conversion statistics based upon interpreting your log files or through including a JavaScript tracking code on your site.

Ad networks are a game of margins. Marketers who track user

action will have a distinct advantage over those who do not.

See also:

- Google Analytics: Google's free analytics program
- Conversion Ruler: a simple, cheap, Web-based analytic tool
- ClickTracks: downloadable, Web-based analytics software

Anchor Text

The text that a user would click on to follow a link. If the link is an image, the image/alt attribute may act in the place of anchor text.

Search engines assume that your page is authoritative for the words that people include in links pointing at your site. When links occur naturally, they typically have a wide array of anchor text combinations. Too much similar anchor text may be considered a sign of manipulation, and thus discounted or filtered. Make sure when you are building links that you control that you try to mix up your anchor text.

Example of anchor text: <a href="http://www.seobook. com/">Search Engine Optimization Blog</a>

Outside of your core brand terms, if you are targeting Google, you probably do not want any more than 10 to 20 percent of your anchor text to be the same. You can use Backlink Analyzer to compare the anchor text profile of other top-ranked competing sites.

See also: Backlink Analyzer **(http://tools.seobook.com/backlink-analyzer/)** — free tool to analyze your link anchor text

B

Backlink (see Inbound Link)

Black Hat SEO

Search engines set up guidelines that help them extract billions of dollars of ad revenue from the work of publishers and the attention of searchers. Within that highly profitable framework, search engines consider certain marketing techniques deceptive in nature, and label them as Black Hat SEO. Those considered within their guidelines are called White Hat SEO techniques. The search guidelines are not a static set of rules, and things that may be considered legitimate one day may be considered deceptive the next.

Search engines are not without flaws in their business models, but there is nothing immoral or illegal about testing search algorithms to understand how search engines work.

People who have extensively tested search algorithms are probably more competent and more knowledgeable search marketers than those who give themselves the arbitrary label of White Hat SEOs while calling others Black Hat SEOs.

When making large investments in processes that are not entirely clear, trust is important. Rather than looking for reasons to not work with an SEO, it is best to look for signs of trust in a person you would like to work with.

See also:

- **BlackHatSEO.com:** parody site about Black Hat SEO
- **WhiteHatSEO.com:** parody site about White Hat SEO
- **SEOConsultants.com:** reviewed directory of SEO professionals

Block Level Analysis

A method used to break a page down into multiple points on the Web graph by breaking its pages down into smaller blocks.

Block level link analysis can be used to help determine whether content is page specific or part of a navigational system. It also can help determine whether a link is a natural editorial link, what other links that link should be associated with, and whether it is an advertisement. Search engines generally do not want to count advertisements as votes.

Blog

A periodically updated journal, typically formatted in reverse chronological order. Many blogs not only archive and categorize information, but also provide a feed and allow simple user interaction, like leaving comments on the posts.

Most blogs tend to be personal in nature. Blogs are generally quite authoritative with heavy link equity because they give people a reason to frequently come back to their site, read their content, and link to whatever they think is interesting. The most popular blogging platforms are Wordpress™, Blogger, Movable Type™, and Typepad™.

Blogger

Blogger is a free blog platform owned by Google. It allows you to publish sites on a subdomain off of **www.blogspot.com**, or to FTP content to your own domain. If you are serious about building a brand or making money online, you should publish your content to your own domain because it can be hard to reclaim a Web site's link equity and age-related trust if you have built years of link equity into a subdomain on someone else's Web site. Blogger is probably the easiest blogging software tool to use, but it lacks some features present in other blog platforms.

Bold

A way to make words appear in a darker font. Words that appear in a bolder font are more likely to be read by humans that are scanning a page. A search engine may also place slightly greater weighting on these words than regular text, but if you write natural page copy, and a word or phrase appears on a page many times, it probably does not make sense or look natural if you bold every occurrence. Example use: words

Bookmarks

Most browsers come with the ability to bookmark your favorite pages. Many web-based services have also been created to allow you to bookmark and share your favorite resources. The popularity of a document (as measured in terms of link equity, number of bookmarks, or usage data) is a signal for the quality of the information. Some search engines may eventually use bookmarks to help aid their search relevancy.

Social bookmarking sites are often called tagging sites. Del.icio. us is the most popular social bookmarking site. Yahoo! MyWeb also allows you to tag results. Google allows you to share feeds and/or tag pages. They also have a program called Google Notebook, which allows you to write mini guides of related links and information.

There are also a few META news sites that allow you to tag interesting pages. If enough people vote for your story, then your story gets featured on the homepage. Slashdot is a tech news site primarily driven by central editors. Digg created a site covering the same type of news, but is a bottoms up news site, which allows readers to vote for what they think is interesting. Netscape cloned the Digg business model and content model. Sites like Digg and Netscape are easy sources of links if you can create content that would appeal to those audiences.

See also:

- Del.icio.us: Yahoo!-owned social bookmarking site
- Yahoo! MyWeb: similar to Del.icio.us, but more integrated into Yahoo!
- Google Notebook: allows you to note documents
- Slashdot: tech news site where stories are approved by central editors
- Digg: decentralized news site
- Netscape: Digg clone
- Google Video: Google's video hosting, tagging, and search site
- YouTube: popular decentralized video site

Breadcrumb Navigation

Navigational technique used to help search engines and Web site users understand the relationship between pages. Example breadcrumb navigation: Home > SEO Tools > SEO for Firefox. Whatever page the user is on is unlinked, but the pages above it within the site structure are linked to, and organized starting with, the home page, right on down through the site structure.

Broken Link

A hyperlink that is not functioning. A link that does not lead to the desired location. Links may be broken for a number of reasons, but four of the most common reasons are a Web site going offline, linking to content which is temporary in nature (due to licensing structures or other reasons), moving a page's location, and changing a domain's content management system. Most large Web sites have some broken links, but if too many of a site's links are broken, it may be an indication of outdated content, and it may provide Web site users with a poor user experience — both of which may cause search engines to rank a page as being less relevant. Xenu Link Sleuth is a free software program, which crawls Web sites to find broken links.

C

Cache

Copy of a Web page stored by a search engine. When you search the Web, you are not actively searching the whole Web, but are searching files in the search engine index.

Some search engines provide links to cached versions of pages in their search results, and allow you to strip some of the formatting from cached copies of pages.

Canonical URL

Many content management systems are configured with errors that cause duplicate or exceptionally similar content to get indexed under multiple URLs. Many Webmasters use inconsistent link structures throughout their site that cause the exact same content to get indexed under multiple URLs. The canonical version of any

URL is the single most authoritative version indexed by major search engines. Search engines typically use PageRank or a similar measure to determine which version of a URL is the canonical URL.

Webmasters should use consistent linking structures throughout their sites to ensure they funnel the maximum amount of PageRank at the URLs they want indexed. When linking to the root level of a site or a folder index, it is best to end the link location at a "/" instead of placing the index.html or default.asp filename in the URL.

Examples of URLs that may contain the same information in spite of being at different Web addresses:

- www.seobook.com/
- www.seobook.com/index.shtml
- http://seobook.com/
- http://seobook.com/index.shtml
- www.seobook.com/?tracking-code

Catalog (see Index)

Catch All Listing

A listing used by pay-per-click search engines to monetize long tail terms that are not yet targeted by marketers. This technique may be valuable if you have very competitive key words, but is not ideal since most major search engines have editorial guidelines that prevent bulk untargeted advertising, and most of the places that allow catch-all listings have low traffic quality. Catch-all listings may be an attractive idea on theme-specific search engines and directories, though, as they are already prequalified clicks.

CGI

Common Gateway Interface — interface software between a Web server and other machines or software running on that server. Many cgi programs are used to add interactivity to a Web site.

Cloaking

Displaying different content to search engines and searchers. Depending on the intent of the display discrepancy and the strength of the brand of the person/company cloaking, it may be considered reasonable or it may get a site banned from a search engine.

Cloaking has many legitimate uses that are within search guidelines. For example, changing user experience based on location is common on many popular Web sites. See also:

- *The Definitive Guide to Cloaking:* Dan Kramer's guide to cloaking
- CloakIt: cheaply priced cloaking software
- Fantomaster: more expensive cloaking software
- *Cluetrain Manifesto:* The book about how the Web is a

marketplace, and how it is different from traditional offline business

Clustering

In search results, the listings from any individual site are typically limited to a certain number and grouped together to make the search results appear neat and organized and to ensure diversity among the top-ranked results. Clustering can also refer to a technique which allows search engines to group hubs and authorities on a specific topic together to further enhance their value by showing their relationships.

See also: Google Touchgraph: interesting Web application that shows the relationship between sites Google returns as being related to a site you enter.

CMS

Content Management System. Tool used to help make it easy to update and add information to a Web site. Blog software programs are some of the most popular content management systems currently used on the Web. Many content management systems have errors associated with them, which make it hard for search engines to index content due to issues such as duplicate content.

Comments Tag

Some Web developers also place comments in the source code

of their work to help make it easy for people to understand the code. HTML comments in the source code of a document appear as <!-- your comment here -->. They can be viewed if someone types the source code of a document, but do not appear in the regular formatted HTML rendered version of a document. In the past, some SEOs would stuff keywords in comment tags to help increase the page keyword density, but search has evolved beyond that stage, and at this point, using comments to stuff keywords into a page adds to your risk profile and presents little ranking upside potential.

Conceptual Links

Links that search engines attempt to understand, beyond just the words in them. Some rather advanced search engines are attempting to find out the concept links versus just matching the words of the text to that specific word set. Some search algorithms may even look at co-citation and words near the link instead of just focusing on anchor text.

Concept Search

A search that attempts to conceptually match results with the query — not necessarily with those words, rather their concept.

For example, if a search engine understands a phrase to be related to another word or phrase, it may return results relevant to that other word or phrase even if the words you searched for are not directly associated with a result. In addition, some search engines will place various types of vertical search results at the top of the search results based on implied query related intent or prior search patterns by you or other searchers.

Contextual Advertising

Advertising programs that generate relevant advertisements based on the content of a Web page. Google AdSense is the most popular contextual advertising program.

Conversion

Many forms of online advertising are easy to track. A conversion is reached when a desired goal is completed. Most offline ads have been much harder to track than online ads. Some marketers use custom phone numbers or coupon codes to tie offline activity to online marketing. Here are a few common examples of desired goals:

- A product sale
- Completing a lead form
- A phone call
- Capturing an e-mail
- Filling out a survey
- Getting a person to pay attention to you
- Getting feedback
- Having a site visitor share your Web site with a friend

- Having a site visitor link at your site

- Bid management, affiliate tracking, and analytics programs make it easy to track conversion sources

See also:

- Google Conversion University: free conversion tracking information

- Google Web site Optimizer: free multi-variable testing product offered by Google.

Copyright

The legal rights to publish and reproduce a particular piece of work. See also: **Copyright.gov**.

Cookie

Small data file written to a user's local machine to track them. Cookies are used to help Web sites customize your user experience and help affiliate program managers track conversions.

Crawl Depth

How deeply a Web site is crawled and indexed. Since searches that are longer in nature tend to be more targeted in nature, it is important to try to get most or all of a site indexed such that the deeper pages have the ability to rank for relevant long tail keywords. A large site needs adequate link equity to get deeply indexed. Another thing that may prevent a site from being fully indexed is duplicate content issues.

Crawl Frequency

How frequently a Web site is crawled. Sites that are well-trusted or frequently updated may be crawled more frequently than sites with low trust scores and limited link authority. Sites with highly artificial link authority scores (i.e., mostly low-quality, spammy links) or sites that are heavy in duplicate content or near duplicate content (such as affiliate feed sites) may be crawled less frequently than sites with unique content that are well integrated into the Web.

CSS

Cascading Style Sheets is a method for adding styles to Web documents. Note: Using external CSS files makes it easy to change the design of many pages by editing a single file. You can link to an external CSS file using code similar to the following in the head of your HTML documents

```
<link rel="stylesheet" href="http://www.seobook.com/style.css" type="text/css" />
```

See also:

- W3C (**www.w3.org**): CSS: official guidelines for CSS

- CSS Zen Garden (**www.csszengardens.com**): examples of various CSS layouts

- **Glish.com:** examples of various CSS layouts, links to other CSS resources

CTR

Click-through rate. The percentage of people who click on an advertisement they viewed, which is a way to measure how relevant a traffic source or keyword is. Search ads typically have a higher click-through rate than traditional banner ads due to being highly relevant to implied searcher demand.

Cybersquatting

Registering domains related to other trademarks or brands in an attempt to cash in on the value created by said trademark or brand.

D

Dead Link

A link that is no longer functional. Most large, high-quality Web sites have at least a few dead links in them, but the ratio of good links to dead links can be seen as a sign of information quality.

Deep Link

A link that points to an internal page within a Web site. When links grow naturally, most high-quality Web sites have many links pointing at interior pages. When you request links from other Web sites, it makes sense to request a link from their most targeted relevant page to your most targeted relevant page. Some Web masters even create content based on easy linking opportunities they think up.

Dedicated Server

Server that is limited to serving one Web site or a small collection of Web sites owned by a single person. Dedicated servers tend to be more reliable than shared (or virtual) servers. Dedicated servers usually run between $100 to $500 a month. Virtual servers typically run between $5 to $50 per month.

Deep Link Ratio

The ratio of links pointing to internal pages to overall links pointing at a Web site. A high deep link ratio is typically a sign of a legitimate natural link profile.

De-Listing

Temporarily or permanently becoming de-indexed from a directory or search engine. De-indexing may be due to any of the following:

- Pages on new Web sites (or sites with limited link authority relative to their size) may be temporarily de-indexed until the search engine does a deep spidering and re-cache of the web.

- During some updates, search engines readjust crawl priorities.

- You need a significant number of high-quality links to get a large Web site well indexed and keep it well indexed.

- Duplicate content filters, inbound and outbound link quality, or other information quality related issues may also relate to re-adjusted crawl priorities.

- Pages that have changed location and are not properly redirected, or pages that are down when a search engine tries to crawl them may be temporarily de-indexed.

Digg

Social news site where users vote on which stories get the most exposure and become the most popular. See also: **www.digg. com**.

Directory

A categorized catalog of Web sites, typically manually organized by topical editorial experts. Some directories cater to specific niche topics, while others are more comprehensive in nature. Major search engines likely place significant weight on links from DMOZ and the Yahoo! Directory. Smaller and less established general directories likely pull less weight. If a directory does not exercise editorial control over listings, search engines will not be likely to trust their links at all.

DMOZ

The Open Directory Project is the largest human-edited directory of Web sites. DMOZ is owned by AOL, and is primarily run by volunteer editors. See also: **DMOZ.org**.

DNS

Domain Name Server or Domain Name System. A naming scheme mechanism used to help resolve a domain name / host name to a specific TCP/IP Address.

Domain

Scheme used for logical or location organization of the web. Many people also use the word domain to refer to a specific Web site.

Doorway Pages

Pages designed to rank for highly targeted search queries, typically designed to redirect searchers to a page with other advertisements. Some Web masters cloak thousands of doorway pages on trusted domains, and rake in a boatload of cash until they are caught and de-listed. If the page would have a unique purpose outside of search, then search engines are generally fine with it, but if the page only exists because search engines exist, then search engines are more likely to frown on the behavior.

Dreamweaver

Popular Web development and editing software offering a what-you-see-is-what-you-get interface.

Duplicate Content

Content that is duplicate or near duplicate in nature. Search engines do not want to index multiple versions of similar content. For example, printer-friendly pages may be search engine unfriendly duplicates. Also, many automated content generation techniques rely on recycling content, so some search engines are somewhat strict in filtering out content they deem to be similar or nearly duplicate in nature.

Dynamic Content

Content that changes over time or uses a dynamic language, such as PHP, to help render the page. In the past, search engines were less aggressive at indexing dynamic content than they currently are. While they have greatly improved their ability to index dynamic content, it is still preferable to use URL rewriting to help make dynamic content look static in nature.

Dynamic Languages

Programming languages, such as PHP or ASP, which build Web pages on the fly upon request.

E

Earnings Per Click

Many contextual advertising publishers estimate their potential earnings based on how much they make from each click.

Editorial Link

Search engines count links as votes of quality. They primarily want to count editorial links that were earned over links that were bought or bartered. Many paid links, such as those from quality directories, still count as signs of votes as long as they are also associated with editorial quality standards. If they are from sites without editorial control, like link farms, they are not likely to help you rank well. Using an algorithm similar to TrustRank, some search engines may place more trust on well known sites with strong editorial guidelines.

Emphasis

An HTML tag used to emphasize text. Please note that it is more important that copy reads well to humans than any boost you may think you will get by tweaking it for bots. If every occurrence of a keyword on a page is in emphasis, that will make the page hard to read, convert poorly, and may look weird to search engines and users alike. emphasis would appear as emphasis.

Entry Page

The page on which a user enters your site. If you are buying pay-per-click ads, it is important to send visitors to the most appropriate and targeted page associated with the keyword they searched for. If you are doing link building, it is important to point links at your most appropriate page when possible, such that if anyone clicks the link, they are taken to the most appropriate and relevant page.

Ethical SEO

Search engines like to paint SEO services that manipulate their relevancy algorithms as being unethical. Any particular technique is not typically associated with ethics, but is either effective or ineffective. Some search marketers lacking in creativity tend to describe services sold by others as being unethical, while their own services are ethical.

Two of the bigger frauds are 1) Not disclosing risks: Some SEOs may use high-risk techniques when they are not needed. Some may make that situation even worse by not disclosing potential risks to clients. 2) Taking money and doing nothing: Since selling SEO services has almost no start-up costs, many of the people selling services may not know how to competently provide them.

Some shady people claim to be SEOs and bilk money out of unsuspecting small businesses. As long as the client is aware of potential risks, there is nothing unethical about being aggressive.

External Link

Link that references another domain. Some people believe in link hoarding, but linking out to other related resources is a good way to help search engines understand what your site is about. If you link out to many low-quality sites or primarily rely on low-quality reciprocal links, some search engines may not rank your site very well. Search engines are more likely to trust high-quality editorial links (both to and from your site).

F

Fair Use

The stated exceptions of allowed usage of work under copyright without requiring permission of the original copyright holder. Fair use is covered in section 107 of the Copyright code. See also: US Copyright Office Section 107.

Feed

Many content management systems, such as blogs, allow readers to subscribe to content update notifications via RSS or XML feeds. Feeds can also refer to pay-per-click syndicated feeds or merchant product feeds. Merchant product feeds have become less effective as a means of content generation due to improving duplicate content filters.

Feed Reader

Software or Web site used to subscribe to feed update notifications.

See also:

- Bloglines: popular Web-based feed reader
- Google Reader: popular Web-based feed reader
- My Yahoo!: allows you to subscribe to feed updates
- FeedDemon: desktop-based feed reader

FFA

"Free for all" pages are pages that allow anyone to add a link to them. Generally, these links do not pull much weight in search relevancy algorithms because many automated programs fill these pages with links pointing at low-quality Web sites.

Filter

Certain activities or signatures that make a page or site appear unnatural might make search engines inclined to filter/remove them out of the search results. For example, if a site publishes significantly duplicated content, it may get a reduced crawl priority and get filtered out of the search results. Some search engines also have filters based on link quality, link growth rate, and anchor text. Some pages are also penalized for spamming.

Flash

Vector graphics-based animation software. This makes it easier to create Web sites that are rich and interactive in nature. Search engines tend to struggle while indexing and ranking flash Web sites because flash typically contains so little relevant content. If you use flash, ensure:

- You embed flash files within HTML pages
- You use a no-embed element to describe what is in the flash
- You publish your flash content in multiple separate files such that you can embed appropriate flash files in relevant pages

Forward Links (see Outbound Links)

Frames

A technique created by Netscape used to display multiple smaller pages on a single display. This Web design technique allows for consistent site navigation, but makes it hard to deep link at relevant content. Given the popularity of server side includes, content management systems, and dynamic languages, there is no legitimate reason to use frames to build a content site today.

Fresh Content

Content that is dynamic in nature and gives people a reason to keep paying attention to your Web site. Many SEOs talk up fresh content, but fresh content does not generally mean re-editing old content. It more often refers to creating new content. The primary advantages to fresh content are:

- Maintaining and growing mindshare: If you keep giving people a reason to pay attention to you, more and more people will pay attention to you, and link to your site.

- Faster idea spreading: If many people pay attention to your site, when you come out with good ideas, they will spread quickly.

- Growing archives: If you are a content producer, then owning more content means you have more chances to rank. If you keep building additional fresh content, eventually, that gives you a large catalog of relevant content.

- Frequent crawling: Frequently updated Web sites are more likely to be crawled frequently.

FTP

File Transfer Protocol is a protocol for transferring data between computers. Many content management systems (such as blogging platforms) include FTP capabilities. Web development software, such as Dreamweaver, also comes with FTP capabilities. There are also a number of free or cheap FTP programs such as Cute FTP, Core FTP, and Leech FTP.

G

Google

The world's leading search engine in terms of reach. Google pioneered search by analyzing linkage data via PageRank. Google was created by Stanford students Larry Page and Sergey Brin.

Google Base

Free database of semantically structured information created by Google. Google Base may also help Google better understand what types of information are commercial in nature, and how they should structure different vertical search products.

Google Bombing

Making a page rank well for a specific search query by pointing hundreds or thousands of links at it with the keywords in the anchor text.

Google Bowling

Knocking a competitor out of the search results by pointing

hundreds or thousands of low-trust, low-quality links at their Web site. Typically, it is easier to bowl new sites out of the results. Older, established sites are much harder to knock out of the search results.

Google Checkout

Payment service provided by Google that helps Google better understand merchant conversion rates and the value of different keywords and markets.

Google Keyword Tool

Keyword research tool provided by Google that estimates the competition for a keyword, recommends related keywords, and will tell you what keywords Google thinks are relevant to your site or a page on your site.

Google Sitemaps

Program that Web masters can use to help Google index their contents. Please note that the best way to submit your site to search engines and to keep it in their search indexes is to build high-quality editorial links. See also: Google Webmaster Central — access to Google Sitemaps and other Web master related tools.

Google Sitelinks

On some search results where Google thinks one result is far more relevant than other results (like navigational or brand related searches), they may list numerous deep links to that site at the top of the search results.

Google Supplemental Index

Index where pages with lower trust scores are stored. Pages may be placed in Google's Supplemental Index if they consist largely of duplicate content, if the URLs are excessively complex in nature, or the site that hosts them lacks significant trust.

H

Headings

The heading element briefly describes the subject of the section it introduces. Heading elements go from H1 to H6, with the lower numbered headings being most important. You should only use a single H1 element on each page, and may want to use multiple other heading elements to structure a document. An H1 element source would look like: <h1>Your Topic</h1>. Heading elements may be styled using CSS. Many content management systems place the same content in the main page heading and the page title, although in many cases, it may be preferential to mix them up if possible. See also: W3C: Headings

Hidden Text

SEO technique used to show search engine spiders text that human visitors do not see. While some sites may get away with it for a while, generally, the risk to reward ratio is inadequate for most legitimate sites to consider using hidden text.

Hijacking

Making a search engine believe that another Web site exists at your URL. Typically done using techniques such as a 302 redirect or META refresh.

Home Page

The main page on your Web site, which is largely responsible for helping develop your brand and setting up the navigational schemes that will be used to help users and search engines navigate your Web site. As far as SEO goes, a home page is typically going to be one of the easier pages to rank for some of your more competitive terms, largely because it is easy to build links at a home page. You should ensure your homepage stays focused and reinforces your brand though, and do not assume that most of your visitors will come to your site via the home page. If your site is well structured, many pages on your site will likely be far more popular and rank better than your home page for relevant queries.

HTML

HyperText Markup Language is the language in which pages on the World Wide Web are created. Some newer Web pages are also formatted in XHTML.

HTTP

HyperText Transfer Protocol is the foremost used protocol to communicate between servers and Web browsers. Hypertext transfer protocol is the means by which data is transferred from its residing location on a server to an active browser.

Hubs

Topical hubs are sites that link to well-trusted sites within their topical community. A topical authority is a page that is referenced from many topical hub sites. A topical hub is a page that references many authorities.

I

Inbound Link

Link pointing to one Web site from another. Most search engines allow you to see a sample of links pointing to a document by searching using the link: function. For example, typing link: **www. seobook.com** into Google and clicking "search" would show pages linking to the home page of this site (both internal links and inbound links). Due to canonical URL issues, **www.site.com** and **site.com** may show different linkage data. Google typically shows a much smaller sample of linkage data than competing engines do, but Google still knows of and counts many of the links that do not show up when you use their link: function.

Index

Collection of data used as bank to search through to find a match to a user-fed query. The larger search engines have billions of documents in their catalogs. When search engines search, they search via reverse indexes by words and return results based on matching relevancy vectors. Stemming and semantic analysis allow search engines to return near matches. Index may also refer to the root of a folder on a web server.

Internal Link

Link from one page on a site to another page on the same site. It is preferential to use descriptive internal linking to make it easy for search engines to understand what your Web site is about. Use consistent navigational anchor text for each section of your site, emphasizing other pages within that section. Place links to relevant related pages within the content area of your site to help further show the relationship between pages and improve the usability of your Web site.

Information Architecture

Designing, categorizing, organizing, and structuring content in a useful, meaningful way. Good information architecture considers how both humans and search spiders access a Web site. Information architecture suggestions:

- Focus each page on a specific topic

- Use descriptive page titles and META descriptions which describe the content of the page

- Use clean (few or no variables) descriptive file names and folder names

- Use headings to help break up text and semantically structure a document

- Use breadcrumb navigation to show page relationships

- Use descriptive link anchor text

- Link to related information from within the content area of your web pages

- Improve conversion rates by making it easy for people to take desired actions

- Avoid feeding search engines duplicate or near-duplicate content

Information Retrieval

The field of science based on sorting or searching through large data sets to find relevant information.

Invisible Web

Portions of the web which are not easily accessible to crawlers due to search technology limitations, copyright issues, or information architecture issues.

IP Address

Internet Protocol Address. Every computer connected to the Internet has an IP address. Some Web sites and servers have unique IP addresses, but most web hosts host multiple Web sites on a single host. Many SEOs refer to unique C class IP addresses. Every site is hosted on a numerical address, like aa.bb.cc.dd. In some cases, many sites are hosted on the same IP address. It is believed by many SEOs that if links come from different IP ranges with a different number somewhere in the aa.bb.cc part, then the link may count more than links from the same local range and host.

IP delivery (see cloaking)

ISP

Internet Service Providers sell end users access to the Web. Some of these companies also sell usage data to web analytics companies.

Italics (see emphasis)

J

JavaScript

A client-side scripting language that can be embedded into HTML documents to add dynamic features. Search engines do not index most content in JavaScript. In AJAX, JavaScript has been combined with other technologies to make Web pages even more interactive.

K

Keyword

A word or phrase that implies a certain mindset or demand that targeted prospects are likely to search for. Long tail and brand-related keywords are typically worth more than shorter and vague keywords because they typically occur later in the buying cycle and are associated with a greater level of implied intent.

Keyword Research

The process of discovering relevant keywords and keyword phrases to focus your SEO and PPC marketing campaigns on. Example keyword discovery methods:

- Using keyword research tools
- Looking at analytics data or your server logs
- Looking at page copy on competing sites
- Reading customer feedback
- Placing a search box on your site and seeing what people are looking for
- Talking to customers to ask how and why they found and chose your business

Keyword Research Tools

Tools that help you discover potential keywords based on past search volumes, search trends, bid prices, and page content from related Web sites. Short list of the most popular keyword research tools:

- SEO Book Keyword Research Tool: Free, driven by Overture, this tool cross references all of my favorite keyword research tools. In addition to linking to traditional keyword research tools, it also links to tools such as Google Suggest, Buzz related tools, vertical databases, social bookmarking and tagging sites, and latent semantic indexing related tools.

- Google: Free, powered from Google search data.

- Wordtracker: Paid, powered from Dogpile and METACrawler. Due to small sample size, their keyword database may be easy to spam.

- Please note that most keyword research tools used alone are going to be highly inaccurate at giving exact quantitative search volumes. The tools are better for qualitative measurements. To test the exact volume for a keyword, it may make sense to set up a test Google AdWords campaign.

Keyword Stuffing

Writing copy that uses excessive amounts of the core keyword. When people use keyword-stuffed copy, it tends to read mechanically (and thus does not convert well and is not link worthy), plus, some pages that are crafted with just the core keyword in mind often lack semantically related words and modifiers from the related vocabulary, which causes the pages to rank poorly as well.

L

Landing Page

The page on which a visitor arrives after clicking on a link or advertisement.

Landing Page Quality Scores

A measure used by Google to help filter noisy ads out of their AdWords program. When Google AdWords launched, affiliates and arbitrage players made up a large portion of their ad market, but as more mainstream companies have spent on search marketing, Google has used many measures to try to keep their ads relevant.

Link

A citation from one Web document to another or to another position in the same document. Most major search engines consider links as a vote of trust.

Link Baiting

The art of targeting, creating, and formatting information that provokes the target audience to point high-quality links at your site. Many link baiting techniques are targeted at social media and bloggers. See also: SEO Book Search: Link Bait

Link Building

The process of building high-quality linkage data that search engines will evaluate to trust your Web site is authoritative, relevant, and trustworthy. A few general link-building tips:

- Build conceptually unique, link-worthy, high-quality content

- Create viral marketing ideas that want to spread and make people talk about you

- Mix your anchor text

- Get deep links

- Try to build at least a few quality links before actively obtaining any low-quality links

- Register your site in relevant high-quality directories such as DMOZ, the Yahoo! Directory, and Business.com

- When possible, try to focus your efforts mainly on getting high-quality editorial links

- Create link bait

- Try to get bloggers to mention you on their blogs

- It takes a while to catch up with the competition, but if you work at it long enough and hard enough, eventually, you can enjoy a self-reinforcing market position

Link Bursts

A rapid increase in the quantity of links pointing at a Web site. When links occur naturally, they generally develop over time. In some cases, it may make sense that popular viral articles receive many links quickly, but in those cases, there are typically other signs of quality as well, such as:

- Increased usage data

- Increase in brand-related search queries

- Traffic from the link sources to the site being linked at

- Many of the new links coming from new pages on trusted domains

Link Churn

The rate at which a site loses links.

Link Equity

A measure of how strong a site is based on its inbound link popularity and the authority of the sites providing those links.

Link Farm

Web site or group of Web sites which exercises little to no editorial control when linking to other sites. FFA pages, for example, are link farms.

Log Files

Server files which show you what your leading sources of traffic are and what people are searching for to find your Web site. Log files do not typically show as much data as analytics programs would, and if they do, it is generally not in a format that is as useful beyond seeing the top few stats.

Link Hoarding

A method of trying to keep all your link popularity by not linking out to other sites, or linking out using JavaScript or through cheesy redirects. Generally, link hoarding is a bad idea for the following reasons:

- Many authority sites were at one point hub sites that freely linked out to other relevant resources

- If you are unwilling to link out to other sites, people are going to be less likely to link to your site

- Outbound links to relevant resources may improve your credibility and boost your overall relevancy scores

Link Popularity

The number of links pointing at a Web site. For competitive search queries, link quality counts much more than link quantity. Google typically shows a smaller sample of known linkage data than the other engines do, even though Google still counts many of the links they do not show when you do a link search.

Link Reputation

The combination of your link equity and anchor text.

Long Tail

Phrase describing how for any category of product being sold, there is much more aggregate demand for the non-hits than there is for the hits. How does the long tail apply to keywords? Long Tail keywords are more precise and specific, thus have a higher value. As of writing this definition in the middle of October 2006, my leading keywords for this month are as follows:

- #reqs search term
    - o   1504 seo book
    - o   512 seobook
    - o   ·501 seo
    - o   214 google auctions
    - o   116 link bait
    - o   95 aaron wall
    - o   94 gmail uk
    - o   89 search engine optimization
    - o   86 trustrank
    - o   78 adsense tracker
    - o   73 latent semantic indexing

- o 71 seo books

- o 69 john t reed

- o 67 dear sir

- o 67 book.com

- o 64 link harvester

- o 64 google adwords coupon

- o 58 seobook.com

- o 55 adwords coupon

- o 15,056 [not listed: 9,584 search terms]

- Notice how the nearly 10,000 unlisted terms account for roughly 10 times as much traffic as I got from my core brand related term (and this site only has a couple thousand pages and has a rather strong brand).

Looksmart

Company originally launched as a directory service which later morphed into a paid search provider and vertical content play. See also: **Looksmart.com**.

LSI

Latent Semantic Indexing is a way for search systems to mathematically understand and represent language based on the similarity of pages and keyword co-occurrence. A relevant result may not even have the search term in it. It may be returned based solely on the fact that it contains many similar words to those appearing in relevant pages which contain the search words. See also:

- Quintura Search: free LSI type keyword research tool

- Patterns in Unstructured Data: free paper describing how LSI works

- SEO Book articles on LSI: No. 1 and No. 2 (Google may not be using LSI, but they are certainly using technologies with similar functions and purpose.)

- Johnon.com Go Words: article about how adding certain relevant words to a page can drastically improve its relevancy for other keywords

M

Manual Review

All major search engines combine a manual review process with their automated relevancy algorithms to help catch search-spam and train their relevancy algorithms. Abnormal usage data or link growth patterns may also flag sites for manual review.

META Description

The META description tag is typically a sentence or two of content that describes the content of the page. A good META description tag should:

- be relevant and unique to the page;

- reinforce the page title; and

- focus on including offers and secondary keywords and phrases to help add context to the page title.

- Relevant META description tags may appear in search results as part of the page description below the page title.

- The code for a META description tag looks like this <META name="Description" content="Your META description here. " / >

- See also: Free META tag generator: offers a free formatting tool and advice on creating META description tags.

META Keywords

The META keywords tag is a tag that can be used to highlight keywords and keyword phrases the page is targeting. The code for a META keyword tag looks like this <META name="Keywords" content="keyword phrase, another keyword, yep another, maybe one more ">. Many people spammed META keyword tags and searchers typically never see the tag, so most search engines do not place much (if any) weight on it. Many SEO professionals no longer use META keywords tags. See also:

- Free META tag generator: offers a free formatting tool and advice on creating META description tags.

N

Navigation

Scheme to help Web site users understand where they are, where they have been, and how that relates to the rest of your Web site. It is best to use regular HTML navigation rather than coding your navigation in JavaScript, Flash, or some other type of navigation that search engines may not be able to easily index.

O

Ontology

In philosophy, it is the study of being. As it relates to search, it is the attempt to create an exhaustive, rigorous conceptual scheme about a domain. An ontology is typically a hierarchical data structure containing all the relevant entities and their relationships and rules within that domain.

Open Source

Software that is distributed with its source code such that developers can modify it as they see fit. On the Web, open source is a great strategy for quickly building immense exposure and mindshare.

Organic Search Results

Most major search engines have results that consist of paid ads and unpaid listings. The unpaid/algorithmic listings are called the organic search results. Organic search results are organized by relevancy, which is largely determined based on linkage data, page content, usage data, and historical domain and trust-related data. Most clicks on search results are on the organic search results. Some studies have shown that 60 to 80 percent of clicks are on the organic search results.

Outbound Link

A link from one Web site pointing at another, external Web site. Some Web masters believe in link hoarding, but linking out to useful relevant related documents is an easy way to help search engines understand what your Web site is about. If you reference other resources, it also helps you build credibility and leverage the work of others without having to do everything yourself. Some Web masters track where their traffic comes from, so if you link to related Web sites, they may be more likely to link back to your site.

P

Page, Larry

Co-founder of Google.

Page Title (see Title)

Paid Inclusion

A method of allowing Web sites that pass editorial quality guidelines to buy relevant exposure. See also:

- Directories such as the Yahoo! Directory and Business.com allow Web sites to be listed for a flat yearly cost.

- Yahoo! Search allows Web masters to pay for inclusion for a flat review fee and a category-based cost per click.

- Paid Link (see Text Link Ads)

Pay for Performance

Payment structure where affiliated sales workers are paid commission for getting consumers to perform certain actions. Publishers publishing contextual ads are typically paid per ad click. Affiliate marketing programs pay affiliates for conversions — leads, downloads, or sales.

Penalty

Search engines prevent some Web sites suspected of spamming from ranking highly in the results by banning or penalizing them. These penalties may be automated algorithmically or manually applied. If a site is penalized algorithmically the site may start ranking again after a certain period of time after the reason for being penalized is fixed. If a site is penalized manually, the penalty may last an exceptionally long time or require contacting the search engine with a re-inclusion request to remedy.

Personalization

Altering the search results based on a person's location, search history, content they recently viewed, or other factors relevant to them on a personal level.

PHP

PHP Hypertext Preprocessor is an open source server side scripting language used to render web pages or add interactivity to them. See also: **www.PHP.net**.

Poison Word

Words traditionally associated with low-quality content that caused search engines to want to demote the rankings of a page. See also: What Are Poison Words? Do They Matter?

PDF

Portable Document Format is a universal file format developed by Adobe Systems that allows files to be stored and viewed in the original printer-friendly context.

Portal

Web site offering common consumer services such as news, e-mail, other content, and search.

PPC

Pay Per Click is a pricing model that most search ads and many contextual ad programs are sold through. PPC ads only charge advertisers if a potential customer clicks on an ad.

See also:

- AdWords: Google's PPC ad platform

- AdCenter: Microsoft's PPC ad platform

- Yahoo! Search Marketing: Yahoo!'s PPC ad platform

Precision

The ability of a search engine to list results that satisfy the query, usually measured in percentage. (If 20 of the 50 results match the query, the precision is 40 percent). Search spam and the complexity of language challenge the precision of search engines.

Profit Elasticity

A measure of the profit potential of different economic conditions based on adjusting price, supply, or other variables to create a different profit potential where the supply and demand curves cross.

Proximity

A measure of how close words are to one another. A page that has words near one another may be deemed to be more likely to satisfy a search query containing both terms. If keyword phrases are repeated an excessive number of times, and the proximity is close on all the occurrences of both words, it may also be a sign of unnatural (and thus potentially low quality) content.

Q

Quality Content

Content that is linkworthy in nature. See also:

- What is Quality Content?

- When Unique Content is Not "Unique"

Quality Link

Search engines count links as votes of trust. Quality links count more than low-quality links. There are a variety of ways to define what a quality link is, but the following are characteristics of a high-quality link:

- Trusted Source: If a link is from a page or Web site that seems like it is trustworthy, then it is more likely to count more than a link from an obscure, rarely used, and rarely cited Web site. See TrustRank for one example of a way to find highly-trusted Web sites.

- Hard to Get: The harder a link is to acquire, the more likely a search engine will be to want to trust it and the more work a competitor will need to do to try to gain that link.

- Aged: Some search engines may trust links from older resources or links that have existed for a length of time more than they trust brand new links or links from newer resources.

- Co-citation: Pages that link at competing sites which also link to your site make it easy for search engines to understand what community your Web site belongs to. See Hilltop for an example of an algorithm that looks for co-citation from expert sources.

- Related: Links from related pages or related Web sites may count more than links from unrelated sites.

- In Content: Links in the content area of a page are typically going to be more likely to be editorial links than links that are not included within the editorial portion of a page.

While appropriate anchor text may also help you rank even better than a link that lacks appropriate anchor text, it is worth noting that for competitive queries, Google is more likely to place weight on a high-quality link where the anchor text does not match than trusting low-quality links where the anchor text matches.

Query

The actual "search string" a searcher enters into a search engine.

Query Refinement

Some searchers may refine their search query if they deemed the results as being irrelevant. Some search engines may aim to promote certain verticals or suggest other search queries if they deem other search queries or vertical databases as being relevant to the goals of the searcher.

Query refinement is both a manual and an automated process. If searchers do not find their search results as being relevant, they may search again. Search engines may also automatically refine queries using the following techniques:

- Google OneBox: promotes a vertical search database near the top of the search result. For example, if image search is relevant to your search query, images may be placed near the top of the search results.

- Spell Correction: offers a did-you-mean link with the

correct spelling near the top of the results.

- Inline Suggest: offers related search results in the search results. Some engines also suggest a variety of related search queries.

Some search toolbars also aim to help searchers auto complete their search queries by offering a list of most popular queries, which match the starting letters that a searcher enters into the search box.

R

Reciprocal Links

Nepotistic link exchanges where Web sites try to build false authority by trading links, using three-way link trades, or using other low-quality link schemes. When sites link naturally, there is going to be some amount of cross-linking within a community, but if most or all of your links are reciprocal in nature, it may be a sign of ranking manipulation. Also, sites that trade links off topic or on links pages that are stashed away deep within their sites probably do not pass much link authority, and may add more risk than reward.

Quality reciprocal link exchanges in and of themselves are not a bad thing, but most reciprocal link offers are of low quality. If too many of your links are of low quality, it may make it harder for your site to rank for relevant queries, and some search engines may look at inlink and outlink ratios as well as link quality when determining how natural a site's link profile is. See also:

- Indexing Timeline: Matt Cutts states that sites which have many low-quality inbound and/or outbound links may struggle to rank or even get deeply indexed by Google.

- Live Search: Linkdomain:SEOBook.com LinkFromDomain: SEOBook.com: shows **SEOBook.com**'s reciprocal links

- What a Link's Page Should Not Look Like: article by Jim Boykin

Redirect

A method of alerting browsers and search engines that a page location moved. 301 redirects are for permanent change of location, and 302 redirects are used for a temporary change of location.

Registrar

A company that allows you to register domain names.

Reinclusion

If a site has been penalized for spamming, they may fix the infraction and ask for reinclusion. Depending on the severity of the infraction and the brand strength of the site, they may or may not be added to the search index. See also:

- Google Reinclusion: sign up for Google Sitemaps, and request reinclusion from within Google Sitemaps

- Yahoo! Reinclusion: request a review here: Yahoo! Search: URL Status: Second Review Request

Referrer

The source from which a Web site visitor came.

Relative Link

A link that shows the relation of the current URL to the URL of the page being linked at. Some links only show relative link paths instead of having the entire reference URL within the "href" tag. Due to canonicalization and hijacking-related issues, it is typically preferred to use absolute links over relative links.

Example relative link: <a href="."./folder/filename.html">Cool Stuff</a>

Example absolute link: <a href="http://seobook.com/folder/filename.html">Cool Stuff</a>

Relevancy

A measure of how useful searchers find search results. Many search engines may also bias organic search results to informational resources since commercial ads also show in the search results.

Reputation Management

Ensuring your brand-related keywords display results that reinforce your brand. Many hate sites tend to rank highly for brand-related queries.

Robots.txt

A file that sits in the root of a site and tells search engines which files not to crawl. Some search engines will still list your URLs as URL only listings even if you block them using a robots.txt file. Do not put files on a public server if you do not want search engines to index them. See also: **Robotstxt.org**.

ROI

Return on Investment is a measure of how much return you receive from each marketing dollar. While ROI is a somewhat sophisticated measurement, some search marketers prefer to account for their marketing using more sophisticated profit elasticity calculations.

RSS

Rich Site Summary or Real Simple Syndication is a method of syndicating information to a feed reader or other software which allows people to subscribe to a channel they are interested in.

S

Search History

Many search engines store user search history information. This data can be used for better ad targeting or to make old information more findable. Search engines may also determine what a document is about and how much they trust a domain based on aggregate usage data. Many brand-related search queries is a strong signal of quality.

SEO

Search engine optimization is the art and science of publishing information and marketing it in a manner that helps search engines understand your information is relevant to relevant search queries. SEO consists largely of keyword research, SEO copywriting, information architecture, link building, brand building, building mindshare, reputation management, and viral marketing.

SEO Copywriting

Writing and formatting copy in a way that will help make the documents appear relevant to a wide array of relevant search queries. There are two main ways to write titles and be SEO friendly:

- Write literal titles that are well aligned with things people search for. This works well if you need backfill content for your site or already have an amazingly authoritative site.

- Write page titles that are exceptionally compelling to link at. If enough people link at them, then your pages and site will rank for many relevant queries even if the keywords are not in the page titles.

Spam

Unsolicited e-mail messages. Search engines also like to outsource their relevancy issues by calling low-quality search results spam. They have vague, ever-changing guidelines that determine what marketing techniques are acceptable at any given time. Typically, search engines try hard not to flag false positives as spam, so most algorithms are quite lenient, as long as you do not build many low-quality links, host large quantities of duplicate content, or perform other actions that are considered widely outside of relevancy guidelines. If your site is banned from a search engine, you may request reinclusion after fixing the problem.

See also:

Google Web master Guidelines

Microsoft Live Search: Guidelines for successful indexing

Yahoo! Search Content Quality Guidelines

BMW Spamming: Matt Cutts posted about BMW using search spam. Due to their brand strength, BMW was reincluded in Google quickly.

Spamming: The act of creating and distributing spam.

Spider: Search engine crawlers that search or "spider" the Web for pages to include in the index.

Many non-traditional search companies have different spiders that perform other applications. For example, TurnItInBot searches for plagiarism. Spiders should obey the robots.txt protocol.

Splash Page

Features rich or elegantly designed, beautiful Web page that typically offers poor usability and does not offer search engines much content to index. Make sure your home page has relevant content on it if possible.

Spyware

Software programs that spy on Web users, often used to collect consumer research and to behaviorally targeted ads.

Static Content

Content that does not change frequently. May also refer to content that does not have any social elements to it and does not use dynamic programming languages. Many static sites do well, but the reasons fresh content works great for SEO are:

- If you keep building content every day, you eventually

build a huge archive of content

- By frequently updating your content, you keep building mindshare, brand equity, and give people fresh content worth linking at

T

Text Link Ads

Advertisements that are formatted as text links. Since the Web was originally based on text and links, people are typically more inclined to pay attention to text links than some other ad formats that are typically less relevant and more annoying. However, search engines primarily want to count editorial links as votes, so links that are grouped together with other paid links (especially if those links are to off-topic commercial sites) may be less likely to carry weight in search engines.

Title

The title element is used to describe the contents of a document. The title is one of the most important aspects to doing SEO on a Web page. Each page title should be:

- Unique to that page: Not the same for every page of a site.

- Descriptive: What important ideas does that page cover?

- Not excessively long: Typically, page titles should be kept to eight to ten words or less, with some of the most important words occurring near the beginning of the page title.

- Page titles appear in search results as the links searchers click on. In addition, many people link to documents using the official document title as the link anchor text. Thus, by using a descriptive page title, you are likely to gain descriptive anchor text and are more likely to have your listing clicked on.

Toolbar

Many major search companies aim to gain marketshare by distributing search toolbars. Some of these toolbars have useful features such as pop-up blockers, spell checkers, and form autofill. These toolbars also help search engines track usage data.

TrustRank

Search relevancy algorithm that places additional weighting on links from trusted seed Web sites that are controlled by major corporations, educational institutions, or governmental institutions.

U

Unethical SEO

Some search engine marketers lacking in creativity try to market their services as being ethical, whereas services rendered by other providers are somehow unethical. SEO services are generally neither ethical nor unethical. They are either effective or ineffective. SEO is an inherently risky business, but any quality SEO service provider should make clients aware of potential risks and rewards of different recommended techniques.

Update

Search engines frequently update their algorithms and data sets to help keep their search results fresh and make their relevancy algorithms hard to update. Most major search engines are continuously updating both their relevancy algorithms and search index.

URL

Uniform Resource Locator is the unique address of any Web document.

URL Rewrite

A technique used to help make URLs more unique and descriptive to help facilitate better site-wide indexing by major search engines.

Usability

How easy it is for customers to perform the desired actions. The structure and formatting of text and hyperlink-based calls to action can drastically increase your Web site usability, and thus, conversion rates.

Usage Data

Things like a large stream of traffic, repeat visitors, multiple page views per visitor, a high click-through rate, or a high level of brand-related search queries may be seen by some search engines as a sign of quality.

V

Viral Marketing

Self-propagating marketing techniques. Common modes of transmission are e-mail, blogging, and word-of-mouth marketing channels. Many social news sites and social bookmarking sites also lead to secondary citations.

Virtual Server

A server that allows multiple top-level domains to be hosted from a single computer. Using a virtual server can save money for smaller applications, but dedicated hosting should be used for large commercial platforms. Most domains are hosted on virtual servers, but using a dedicated server on your most important domains should add server reliability, and could be seen as a sign of quality. Dedicated servers usually run between $100 to $500 a month. Virtual servers typically run between $5 to $50 per month.

W

Whois

Each domain has an owner of record. Ownership data is stored in the Whois record for that domain. Some domain registrars also allow you to hide the ownership data of your sites. Many large scale spammers use fake Whois data.

White Hat SEO

Search engines set up guidelines that help them extract billions of dollars of ad revenue from the work of publishers and the attention of searchers. Within that highly profitable framework, search engines consider certain marketing techniques deceptive in nature, and label them as Black Hat SEO. Those which are considered within their guidelines are called White Hat SEO techniques. The search guidelines are not a static set of rules, and things that may be considered legitimate one day may be considered deceptive the next.

Search engines are not without flaws in their business models, but there is nothing immoral or illegal about testing search algorithms to understand how search engines work.

People who have extensively tested search algorithms are probably more competent and more knowledgeable search marketers than those who give themselves the arbitrary label of White Hat SEOs while calling others Black Hat SEOs.

When making large investments in processes that are not entirely clear, trust is important. Rather than looking for reasons to not work with an SEO, it is best to look for signs of trust in a person you would like to work with.

See also:

- **WhiteHatSEO.com**: parody site about White Hat SEO

- **BlackHatSEO.com**: parody site about Black Hat SEO

- **HonestSEO.com**: site offering tips on hiring an SEO

- **SEOConsultants.com**: reviewed directory of SEO professionals

- **SEOBlackHat.com**: blog about Black Hat SEO techniques

Wiki

Software that allows information to be published using collaborative editing.

Wikipedia

Free online collaborative encyclopedia using wiki software. See also: **www.wikipedia.org**.

Wordpress

Popular open source blogging software platform, offering both a downloadable blogging program and a hosted solution. If you are serious about building a brand or making money online, you should publish your content to your own domain because it can be hard to reclaim a Web site's link equity and age-related trust if you have built years of link equity into a sub-domain on someone else's Web site.

See also:

- **www.wordpress.org**: download the software

- **www.wordpress.com**: offers free blog hosting

Wordtracker

Feature-rich paid keyword research tool that collects data from a few popular META search engines, like Dogpile. Due to Wordtracker's small sample size, their data may be easy to manipulate. See also: **www.wordtracker.com**: official site. Digital Point Keyword Suggestion Tool: free keyword research tool that returns keyword research data from Overture and Wordtracker side by side.

X

Xenu Link Sleuth

Popular free software for checking a site for broken internal or external links and creating a sitemap.

XHTML

Extensible HyperText Markup Language is a class of specifications designed to move HTML to conform to XML formatting.

XML

Extensible Markup Language is a simple, very flexible text format derived from SGML, used to make it easy to syndicate or format information using technologies such as RSS.

Resources and Suggested Reading

http://adwords.google.com/support/bin/answer.py?answer=6100

http://b2bnewz.com/content/view/377/42/

http://en.wikipedia.org

http://ezinearticles.com

www.google.com/support/webmasters/bin/answer.py?answer=40318&hl=en

http://tools.seobook.com/backlink-analyzer/

http://tools.seobook.com/keyword-tools/seobook

www.7riversmarketplace.com/SS/Page.aspx?sstarg=&facing=false&secid=62570&artid=1065326

www.uwlax.edu/sbdc/CGBP-Series-2009.htm

www.wigcot.org/index.htm

www.w3.org/WAI/EO/Drafts/PWD-Use-Web/Overview.html

Toolbar.google.com

www.elance.com

www.Google.com/support/googleanalytics/

www.Google.com/support/webmasters/

www.Googlewebmastercentral.blogspot.com

www.IdeaMarketers.com

www.Keyworddiscovery.com/search.html

www.Mozilla.com

www.Seobook.com/seo-firefox-now-seo-x-ray

www.seotrainingproducts.com/tools

www.Xml-sitemaps.com

INDEX

W

X

MORE GREAT TITLES FROM ATLANTIC PUBLISHING

eBay's Secrets Revealed: *The Insider's Guide to Advertising, Marketing, and Promoting Your eBay Store — With Little or No Money*

This book is for those already operating on eBay who want to know how to make more money. Learn dozens of methods to automate your business, including inventory, preventing fraud, payments, accounting, taxes, and fulfillment. Learn new ways to find products and get positive feedback. You will learn pricing strategies, creative methods of writing powerful ad copy that really sells, how to obtain products below wholesale, and ways to make your business work smarter while decreasing your work load.

ISBN-13: 978-0-910627-86-3 • $24.95

The Complete Tax Guide for eBay Sellers: *Insider Secrets You Need to Know*

Learn how to take advantage of legal tax loopholes and how to choose the proper business structure. This book covers everything you will need to know to balance the books, including assets and liabilities, keeping track of transactions, payroll, sales tax, balance sheets, financial statements, operating accounts, and complete tax information.

ISBN-13: 978-1-60138-124-8 • $24.95

eBay Income: *How ANYONE of Any Age, Location and/or Background Can Build a Highly Profitable Online Business with eBay*

"A sound eBay business primer. It not only provides accurate and insightful information on how to sell on eBay, but it goes beyond that to include essential information and resources important for first-time business owners. A must-have for the serious eBay seller." — *James Scurlock, Certified Education Specialist trained by eBay*

ISBN-13: 978-0-910627-58-0 • $24.95

How and Where to Locate the Merchandise to Sell on eBay: *Insider Information You Need to Know from the Experts Who Do It Every Day*

Learn where to find products that you can buy for a few cents on the dollar and resell for massive profits! You will be provided detailed information on wholesalers, drop shippers, closeouts, discontinued merchandise, overstocks, customer returns, liquidators, close out firms, foreign and domestic manufacturers, places to look in your area, and more. You will learn to become a product sourcing pro and make money on eBay! All types of products are covered.

ISBN-13: 978-0-910627-87-0 • $24.95

To order call toll-free **800-814-1132** or visit **www.atlantic-pub.com**